# Brave Parents, Courageous Kids

# Brave Parents, Courageous Kids

Reclaiming Childhood and Releasing World Changers

Dr. Douglas Witherup

ISBN-13: **9780692720264**
ISBN-10: **069272026X**
Interrobang Press, Concord, NC

**What Others are Saying**

*"Doug's distinctive angle on the hidden childhood of David is a fun and practical read for parents who want to raise kids who love Jesus, love life, and live brave."*

—**Chad Veach**, Lead Pastor of Zoe Church and author of *Unreasonable Hope*

"In *Brave Parents, Courageous Kids*, Doug takes aim at one of the most undetected and unchallenged sins in the American church today: the worship of our own children. Anytime our hearts treasure the gift—even the wonderful gift of children—more than the Giver, we find ourselves entrenched in idolatry. The resulting danger to our own emotions and spiritual lives is only rivaled by the potential damage we inflict upon our kids. Doug weaves together stories, research, practical wisdom, and teaching from Scripture in a way that will both challenge you in your shortcomings and offer you hope for a better way forward. As a ministry leader, I am thankful for this book. As a dad to three amazing little girls, I am indebted."

—**David Hertweck**, Youth & Chi Alpha Director for the New York Ministry Network, author of *Good Kids, Big Events & Matching T-Shirts* and *The Word & The Spirit*

*"The overwhelming importance of family is inarguable. I am grateful for the recent emphasis on how the family and the church, in partnership, make healthy disciples. Knowing how to do this, however, is another discussion. If you have good seed, planted in good soil, but an unhealthy environment, you will not bear fruit. Doug Witherup draws attention not only to the importance of the family environment but how to cultivate those planted in it. I endorse this book and the resounding message behind it. If we equip parents with the right tools, the giants standing in our way will have to bow."*

—**Heath Adamson**, National Youth Director of the Assemblies of God and author of *The Bush is Still Burning*

*Dr. Witherup speaks out with bold clarity and courage against the cultural norm in order to produce pure, playful, and powerful results in the hearts of children. In our twenty-three years of pastoral youth ministry and as parents of six children, we agree that focusing on character-building over a child's performance skill set is not only wise but also critical in avoiding modern forms of childhood stress that lead to less than desired outcomes. If applied practically in the decisions and actions of the everyday family, the principles communicated in Brave Parents, Courageous Kids provide freedom to parents who ultimately desire for their children to thrive but find themselves trapped in the unnecessary pressures of pushing them to do too much, too soon.*

—**Scotty and Casey Gibbons**, Scotty is a Teaching Pastor at North Point Church and author of *The Big Ten*, *Carry-on*, and *Overflow*, Casey is a speaker, blogger, and author of *A Girl's Life with God*

*While the macro theme of the book is centered on parenting, Dr. Doug Witherup also illuminates the myths and toxicity of the youth sports culture in America. Too often the Christian community has been unwilling to wrestle with the difficult task of understanding sport and its relationship to our faith, however Brave Parents, Courageous Kids raises questions which we must consider as parents, believers, and sport enthusiasts.*

—**Duane Aagaard**, Ph.D., Professor of Sport Management, Pheiffer University

# Table of Contents

Acknowledgements ............ xiii
Preface ............ xv

**Introduction**
1 The Threat to the Ecosystem of Childhood ............ 1
2 The Myth of The Perfect Crayon Box and other Toxic Parenting Myths ............ 17

**Part I: A Pure Heart- Loving Jesus**
3 A Child Who Loves Jesus ............ 43
4 A Child Who Walks in Anointing ............ 63

**Part II: A Playful Spirit- Having Fun**
5 A Child Who has a Playful Spirit ............ 83
6 A Child Who Chooses Faith-Adventure ............ 99

**Part III: A Powerful Life- Living Brave**
7 A Child Who is Strong ............ 115
8 A Child Who is Courageous ............ 139

Notes ............ 161

*To mom and dad.*
*The field was amazing.*

# ACKNOWLEDGEMENTS

CAMDEN, YOU ARE my very best friend. I'm so glad we get to share life and be parents together.

Cade & Ana, thanks for being such amazing kids. My heart is full watching you guys loving Jesus, having fun, and living courageously.

David Docusen, thanks for being such an amazing friend and encourager. Those conversations at Not Just Coffee infused life into this book.

Lori Wagner (my editor), thank you for asking tough questions. You made me frustrated, but you made me better.

Dr. Duane Aagaard, thank you for your friendship, encouragement, and great discussions on sport and spirituality.

Mary Ritter, thanks for your expertise in the English language. You made my voice stronger.

Elevation Worship, thank you for supplying the soundtrack for some of my writing days. #HereAsInHeaven.

Thank you to my "field-testers," Tracy Breslin, Duane and Katie Aagaard, Jen Boyd, David and Dara Docusen, and Kevin Glenn. Your input and insight have been beyond valuable.

Thank you Gwen Stowers for the small group discussion questions. I believe that as this book is read in community, its true potential will emerge.

# Preface

I didn't want to write this book. Not now, anyways. Ten years ago? Sure. Fifteen years from now? Probably. But not now.

Ten years ago, I considered myself somewhat of a parenting expert. I was a youth pastor who had lots of experience with teenagers and plenty of thoughts about what, in my (not-so)-humble opinion, parents were doing wrong. The only problem was, I had no children of my own. So when my son was born, one of the first things I wanted to do was to go around apologizing to every parent who I had judged for being late to church or for not controlling their crying child in public.

Fast-forward fifteen years from now. At that time, my kids will be 22 and 24. I wholeheartedly desire that they will be finishing college, launching families and careers, loving Jesus, and preparing to change the world. Now *that* would be a great time to write a parenting book—*after* I've seen some success.

But the Lord had different plans. So I'm writing this book now—not as someone who has it figured out, but as a fellow parent in the midst of the daily joys and struggles of raising children. I'm writing as one of you, in the trenches, as a dad who doesn't have it all together but is striving to serve Jesus and raise my children in a way that would be pleasing to him.

I don't mean to be selfish, but the more I wrote this book, the more I thought, "I'm writing this for me." So, if you happen to read and things resonate, I'm happy for you. But if, at the end of the day, I wrote this book for myself, then hopefully and humbly at least I'll be a better dad to Cade and Ana.

I love what filmmaker and author Phil Cooke says: "I don't write books because I have all the answers. I write books because I'm struggling with the questions and searching for solutions."[1] That's me—just a parent who really loves Jesus and my kids and who is asking questions and discovering solutions through God's Word. If you want to come along for the ride, let's go.

# 1

## The Threat to the Ecosystem of Childhood

PARENTS, WHAT DO you want for your children? What are your hopes and dreams for the kind of person they will become? When you drop them off at college their Freshman year, finish arranging the final piece of furniture in their dorm room, and get one last hug while fighting back tears, what qualities and characteristics do you want them to have? What if, as they emerged into adulthood, your children loved Jesus, loved life, and ran with courage into their destiny? Could you want anything more?

These characteristics describe arguably one of the greatest young leaders of one of the greatest nations in history—King David. Most people know David as the man who defeated Goliath, the King of Israel, and the writer of the Psalms. Perhaps not as many are familiar with his boyhood. But, as we will discover, David's childhood provided the crucial environment to produce the young man who was called "a man after God's own heart." As a child in a hidden shepherd's field, David developed a pure heart, a playful spirit, and a powerful life. Your child can too.

---

As a child in a hidden shepherd's field, David developed a pure heart, a playful spirit, and a powerful life. Your child can too.

---

But what if I told you that the pervasive modern-day parenting philosophy is running a bulldozer through the very ecosystem where these qualities are best developed?

## Bulldozing the Ecosystem

The Tropical Andes ecosystem covers a chain of mountain ranges stretching down the west coast of South America from Bolivia to Chile. Although this land area accounts for only one percent of the earth's land mass, its ecosystem is home to one-sixth of all plant life on earth. It has been referred to as the "global epicenter of biodiversity."

If you were to go on an expedition through this area, you would see breathtaking sights—lush tropical rainforests, spectacular waterfalls, and snow-capped mountains. But as is the case with many of our planet's most life-producing ecosystems, the Tropical Andes are in trouble. Roads and pipelines are plowing through sensitive areas. Hydroelectric dams threaten rivers. Forests are being bulldozed. Due to these factors and more, the Tropical Andes are listed among the eight most endangered ecosystems on the planet.

An ecosystem is defined as a community of living organisms in conjunction with the nonliving components of their environment (things like air, water, and soil) interacting as a system. When an ecosystem is intact, it leads to organisms that thrive. But when an ecosystem becomes endangered, it threatens the life, health, and growth of the organisms within that system.

The problem with modern-day parenting is that we're bulldozing the ecosystem of childhood. We're turning sandlots into stadiums, recess into rec leagues, and play into performance. We're organizing the fun out of childhood and in doing so, are squeezing the life out of our kids in the process. I realize these are shocking statements. But before we dive headlong into explanations, allow me to share part of my story.

---

We're bulldozing the ecosystem of childhood. We're turning sandlots into stadiums, recess into rec leagues, and play into performance. We're organizing the fun out of childhood and in doing so, are squeezing the life out of our kids in the process.

---

## My Story

I wish I could point fingers and blame a lot of external factors for bulldozing the ecosystem of my own kids' lives. But I can't. Because I found out the hard way that I've got a bulldozer inside of *me*.

At the time of writing, my job and ministry involved leading the church ministries portfolio for over 300 churches for my denomination in North Carolina. Part of that job was helping to lead hundreds of church leaders and putting on events for thousands of people. A while back, however, it wasn't the biggest stressor in my life. Not even close. What was? Being an assistant coach on my seven-year-old son's baseball team. I know, it sounds ridiculous. But it was true. I wasn't stressed over ministry or leadership. I was stressed over Little League.

Allow me to explain. The league we played in has a fair process of dividing up players of varying skill level across different teams to ensure that the teams will be as equal as possible. For whatever reason, that particular year it didn't work. And when I say it didn't work, I mean it really didn't work. When we had our first practice, I already had a hunch that we would be in for a long season. Some of the basic skills like how to throw and catch that should have been beginning to develop by that age weren't there. Our team was young and small. "This is going to be a tough season," I thought.

After a couple of practices, my stress escalated. This time, it didn't have anything to do with our team. I made the mistake of watching *another* team practice. Baseballs were actually being thrown to other individuals instead of wide-open spaces. Kids were catching the ball instead of writing in the infield dirt. They were hitting the ball instead of looking like a cross between spinning ballerinas and wood-chopping lumberjacks at the plate. And they were big. Really big. (Would it be weird to ask our Little League president to test players for performance enhancing drugs?)

That's when I started to compare. We weren't just going to lose; we were going to get crushed. I tried to psyche myself up by thinking of epic underdog kids' sports movies: *The Bad News Bears. The Mighty Ducks. Sandlot. Kicking and Screaming.* That was it!

But who was I kidding? That was the movies; this was real life.

From there the downward spiral tightened. I began to have thoughts like, "How would I look? Would I be embarrassed?" It even went beyond the team as a whole to my own son. Even though my seven-year-old was a good little ballplayer, I found myself practicing with him more often. But why? Was I pitching to Cade in the backyard because I wanted him to be better or because I wanted to look better? Was I playing catch with my son because I wanted to spend time with him or to feed my own ego?

It was having less and less to do with the kids and more and more to do with me. Yep, a 40-year-old pastor with a doctoral degree was connecting his self-worth to a Little League Team. How messed-up is that?! Before you roll your eyes at me and recommend that I go for counseling, my hunch is that I'm just one of many parents who find themselves, I believe largely unintentionally, swept up and swept into a performance-based, stage parenting culture.

We see this "stage parenting," or parenting for a skill set, all around us. We see mini-vans and SUV's plastered with stickers of kids' activities and driven around as though they're a billboard of success. We see parents who have become emotional leeches off of their children, drawing their sense achievement and self-worth from their child's accomplishments. We see parents who've become more concerned with their child's social status than their child's spiritual status.

Perhaps you've even experienced it to one degree or another in your own life. For instance, have you ever rolled your eyes at over-the-top "stage parents" but secretly worried that your child was somehow be falling behind? Have you ever looked at the family calendar and wondered when things got out of control? Have you ever felt pressure to get your child involved in some activity (dance, karate, soccer, baseball, etc.) out of fear they needed to develop that particular skill set at an early age to compete? Have you ever found yourself comparing your child (reading level, athletic ability, behavior) to other children? Have you ever tied your sense of self-worth to your child's performance? If you found yourself reluctantly nodding your head in the affirmative to one (or all) of those questions, believe me, you're not alone. Somehow in our quest to want to "more" and "better" for our children, we seem to have forgotten the beauty of letting kids actually have a childhood.

Speaking of childhood, remember those days? Remember carefree days of sunshine, summer, and swimming? Remember days in the backyard of riding bikes and building forts? These are exactly the things we're running a bulldozer through. Allow me to explain.

## THE BULLDOZER OF STAGE PARENTING

The destruction of the ecosystem of childhood is the result of what we will refer to as "Stage Parenting." Up until the 1960's, an American childhood was largely a time of fun and freedom, and parents focused on developing a child's character. Kids were taught things like respect, manners, and obedience. But in the 1960's, a parenting philosophy came to prominence that changed the focus from developing the child's character to developing the child's skill set. Our culture began to center on things like getting our kids into the best schools, the most gifted academic programs, and the best traveling sports teams. We began jockeying to have them coached by the best coaches and taught by the most prestigious voice and dance instructors. We began to push our kids further and further, faster and faster, at a younger and younger age in academics, athletics, and the arts, thinking we were setting them up for success. Unfortunately, while the intention may have been to see the child succeed, the philosophy ended up robbing children of the very ecosystem needed for success—a childhood.

Within this stage parenting philosophy, there are three primary elements:

1) Helicopter Parents- parents who hover, cover, and smother, all in the name of wanting what's best for their child
2) Trophy Children- children who have become their parents' "masterpiece"[1]
3) Child Idolatry- the centering of the home (including schedule and finances) around the "development" of the child

Stage Parenting has resulted in stressed-out parents who run their kids from practice to practice and event to event, producing children who never learn self-reliance, and who are therefore not released into the fullness of their future. We don't need a parenting adjustment. We need a parenting revolution. It can come. And it can come through you.

---

We don't need a parenting adjustment. We need a parenting revolution.

---

I believe the majority of parents struggling with these issues are good people who want the best for their children, yet have been caught up in a system that has overtaken us. It's like swimming in a fast-moving current in the ocean. We just went out to play in the water with the kids, looked up, realized we were a half-mile down the beach, and wondered what happened. We didn't mean to stray this far. We were just playing in a system that wielded a greater force than we expected. We find ourselves thinking, "This doesn't feel right. However, what choice do we have? If my kid wants to play in the ocean, I guess we'll just have to fight the current." Not so. What if we found a different ocean?

The good news for parents is that the Bible shows us a better way—a way that not only reduces the stress and anxiety of modern parenting, but restores the fun and joy of childhood. Furthermore, it creates an environment where your child can grow and thrive.

In order to discover how to restore the ecosystem, we'll take a journey back to the story of one of the greatest biblical leaders of all time—King David. David's boyhood in the hiddenness of the shepherd's field was a crucial ecosystem that allowed him to emerge as a great young adult. And not only was it a great environment, but David gives us a further glimpse into his boyhood when he later reflects,"O God, you have taught me from my earliest childhood."[2] While David was growing up in the shepherd's field, the Lord himself was teaching and training David. That must have must made for quite a childhood!

In other words,

a great ecosystem + a great God =
a child who emerges a great young adult.

Take a look at that equation. You don't need to remember too much from middle school math to realize that there is one constant and one variable. And here's a hint: God is the constant. So our job as parents is to provide the ecosystem whereby God can do His best work in our kids.

Notice I said, "Provide the ecosystem where *God* does His best work" and not "the perfect ecosystem where we do our best work." I don't know about you, but if I wasn't already aware of my failures, faults, and shortcomings, parenthood has a way of holding a magnifying glass to all of them. As God tells us through the Apostle Paul, "'My grace is sufficient for you, for my power is made perfect in weakness.' Therefore I will boast all the more gladly about my weaknesses, so that Christ's power may rest on me."[3] That's my kind of "parenting verse." As we do our best, in the power and strength of Jesus, to provide a great ecosystem for our kids, God takes over and does the rest.

That's exactly the journey we'll take in this book. We'll examine the childhood of one of the greatest leaders of all time. And you'll be empowered to provide the environment for God to develop your kids into adults who don't just achieve worldly success, but who have kingdom significance. The bulldozers, both internal and external, have come out in full force. However, not only can we stop them; we can rebuild the ecosystem.

## DAVID'S BROTHER'S: THE STAGE

David and his brothers had the same DNA and were raised by the same parents. Yet while his brothers were passed over by Samuel and, as far as we know, never achieved success in life, David was chosen, anointed, and went on to become a giant killer and world changer. What was the difference? The Scripture gives us the key:

> *"The Lord does not look at the things people look at. People look at the outward appearance, but the Lord looks at the heart" (1 Samuel 16:7).*

"Outward appearance" versus "the heart." Sound familiar? Remember the change in parenting philosophy from skill set (outward appearance) to character (heart)? David's brothers were placed "on stage" before Samuel to show off their outward skill set. David grew up in a shepherd's field and developed character. David's brothers were exalted by people but passed over by the Lord. David was overlooked by people but chosen by the Lord. Two different ecosystems produced two drastically different results.

Perhaps you recall the backstory to this event. Israel's need for a new king prompted the Lord to send the prophet Samuel to Jesse's house to find and anoint the heir to the throne. Seeing how "king of the nation" was a pretty desirable position, you can imagine Jesse's excitement. There was most likely some pretty intense preparation and coaching from dad leading up to Samuel's arrival—hair cuts, new clothes, and plenty of good advice like, "Stand up straight son, give a firm handshake, look him in the eye."

Jesse lined up his sons, putting their "outward appearance" on display for the world to see, hoping that one would be discovered and catapulted into fame and success. Do you see what's happening here? Jesse is the first stage parent. There he is, having heard that the "Israel's Got Talent" scouting crew is on its way to his house, and he's got his sons lined up and ready to perform.

Samuel arrived and began to go down the line. It was quite a line up. It was full of good-looking, strong, talented young men. It was the "king-to-be" traveling all-star team. Surely Israel would be fortunate to have any of these boys as their next ruler. But as Samuel went down the line, looking at them one by one, the Lord said "No." *So, how'd that Stage Parenting thing work out for you, Jesse?* The answer is: it didn't. They all got passed over. No record deal. No major league contract. They didn't even get a callback.

If they weren't chosen as king, at least they would be top leaders, right? Perhaps brave warriors or wealthy businessmen? But they weren't. Granted, we are not told a whole lot about David's brothers, but from what scripture does tell us, we know several things:

1) They were identified as "servants of Saul."

Goliath calls David's brothers "servants of Saul." What a demeaning remark. These were Israelites, servants of the Most High God! They were called and chosen. That was their identifying mark. That was their brand. When Goliath called them "servants of Saul," it was a deep insult. Basically, he was saying, "You don't belong to your God. You belong to this cowardly king." Sadly, David's brothers had become servants of men rather than servants of God. Apparently, they had learned that the highest goal in life is to please man instead of having the courage to go against the flow and please God. They had become people pleasers rather than God pleasers.

2) They were negative and focused on the problem.

The Bible records the Israelite army, which included David's brothers, as asking the question, "Have you seen the giant?" Their question revealed their focus. David's brothers were focused on the problem. Their eyes were locked on the obstacle. Our lives become what we focus on and David's brothers were staring at the size of the giant.

---

Our lives become what we focus on.

---

3) They were "terrified and deeply shaken" and "began to run away in fright."

When the opportunity presented itself to fight, to stand up, to become free and become heroes, David's brothers responded by being "terrified and deeply shaken." Apparently David's brothers had never learned to trust God to fight for them and thus, when it came time to stand up with courage, they were living out of a place of fear. The Bible goes on to say, "They ran away in fright." When you don't know how to face obstacles, you spend your life running from problems instead of running toward victory.

4) They missed their opportunity for greatness and lived in resentment and jealousy.

When David arrived on the scene with bread and cheese, David's oldest brother, Eliab, was furious. "What are you doing around here anyway?" he demanded. "What about those few sheep you're supposed to be taking care of? I know about your pride and deceit. You just want to see the battle." Is there anything sadder than someone who has missed out on his calling in life, someone who is living in fear and hiding, lashing out at someone trying to step into God's calling for his own life? We resent people who remind us what we should have been.

Like Jesse, building a stage for our kids can be so alluring. We want them to succeed and excel. We're tempted to jockey for them to get the lead in the play or a certain position on the team. But when you force your children onto a stage, they fall off. The world doesn't need any more kids who are shoved onto stages by parents; it needs young warriors and world changers who are summoned onto platforms by God.

> The world doesn't need any more kids who are shoved onto stages by parents; it needs young warriors and world changers who are summoned onto platforms by God.

## DAVID: THE FIELD

As Samuel went down the line-up to the last brother, he still heard a "no" from God which left him bewildered. Was there another son? "Oh yeah," Jesse replied. "I do have one more. He's out in the field." This turn of events had to be a confidence buster for David. Not only was he the kid who didn't initially make the team, he wasn't even invited to the try out! As the overlooked kid emerges from the hiddenness of a shepherd's field, something amazing takes place.

As David comes in from the field, "The Lord said, 'Rise and anoint him; this is the one.' So Samuel took the horn of oil and anointed him in the presence of his brothers, and from that day on the Spirit of the Lord came powerfully upon David." The Bible goes on to say that "David had great success because the Lord was with him."[4]

Here's the million-dollar question: *What happened in that shepherd's field?* What type of ecosystem contributed to the emergence of such an amazing young adult? Granted, these were largely hidden years in David's life, and while we don't know everything that occurred in this field, we do know some things. And those things are very significant.

1) We know that as he emerged from the shepherd's field, David was called "a man after God's own heart" and was anointed for his future.

2) We know that as he emerged from the shepherd's field, David was described as "ruddy" (having a youthful energy) and had "bright eyes" (having a bright countenance).

3) We know that as he emerged from the shepherd's field, David had already killed a lion and a bear which gave him the courage to run towards Goliath.

A great ecosystem + a great God =

a child who loves Jesus (Acts 13:22).
a child who walks in anointing (1 Samuel 16:12-13).
a child who has a playful spirit (1 Samuel 16:12).
a child who chooses faith-adventure (1 Samuel 17:26).
a child who is strong (1 Samuel 17:36).
a child who is courageous (1 Samuel 17:48).

Parents, take a moment to look over this list. What if, as your child emerged into adulthood, he or she had these qualities? It can happen! The ecosystem that worked for David can still work today. While you're cultivating the field, God is quietly building the stage. When the last nail is in place, and the heart of your child is ready, he will summon him or her upon it. That's how giant killers are raised and kings are called.

## "Home field" Advantage

In sports, you often hear the term, "home field advantage." Playing on your home turf in front of your own fans can give teams a competitive edge. For the Seattle Seahawks, it's the deafening decibel levels of their screaming fans, known as the "12h man." For the Duke Blue Devils, it's the energy created by the "Cameron Crazies." For the Green Bay

Packers, it's visiting teams playing in the sub-zero temperatures of Lambeau Field. The environment at home provides the advantage.

Think of this in terms of David and his childhood. Remember where David was raised: in the hiddenness and obscurity of a shepherd's field. This environment is where David developed into a man after God's own heart. David had the ultimate "home field" advantage.

---

David had the ultimate "home field" advantage.

---

Part of our role as parents is to provide a home field advantage for our kids. Parents, you got this—because God's got this. Get ready to enjoy being a parent again. Get ready to rediscover the beauty and joy of childhood again. And get ready to raise children who, like David, emerge as young adults who love Jesus, have a playful spirit, and run with courage toward their God-given purpose.

---

Parents, you got this—because God's got this. Get ready to enjoy being a parent again. Get ready to rediscover the beauty and joy of childhood again. And get ready to raise children who, like David, emerge as young adults who love Jesus, have a playful spirit, and run with courage toward their God-given purpose.

---

## Group Discussion Guide

1) "Stage parenting" is represented by a bulldozer in the ecosystem of childhood, including the aspects of: helicopter parents, trophy children, and child idolatry. Where have you noticed these elements around you? Where have you noticed them in your own parenting?
2) 2 Corinthians 12:9 states, "'My grace is all you need. My power works best in weakness.' So now I am glad to boast about my weaknesses, so that the power of Christ can work through me." What parenting weaknesses can you "gladly boast" about?
3) When your son or daughter graduates high school, what kind of person do you want him or her to be? What action steps can you take this week to help your child begin to acquire this type of character?

# 2

## The Myth of The Perfect Crayon Box and other Toxic Parenting Myths

I am a typical first-born who, the older I get, is coming to terms with some of my OCD tendencies. I like to be in control, and I prefer things to be neat and organized. When I mow the grass, I want the lines to be nice and straight. When I play with my kids, I want the toy they were playing with put away before we move on to the next. I like pillows in their place on the couch and beds perfectly made. And crayons—well, ideally crayons would always look the way they do right off the shelf.

For someone with my organizational tendencies, there's something quite appealing about a brand-new box of Crayola 64 crayons. They're beautifully organized. All of the points are intact. No paper is ripped. None have yet been broken in half. But there is a major problem with this picture, because perfect crayons in a box only produce a colorless world.

In contrast, my kids' crayon box is a mess. The crayons are dumped in at random, all mixed together. Once grasped in the fingers of my children, the paper is ripped and the points are gone.

Some are chipped and broken. But even in their brokenness, they produce beauty. Depending on the season, our refrigerator is decorated with pictures of Christmas trees, snowflakes, fall leaves, sunsets, princesses, rainbows, Ninja Turtles, and Star Wars. I wouldn't have it any other way. These works of art are produced out of that beautiful mess of broken crayons.

A beautiful mess—that's what my family is. And I bet that's what your family is too.

A beautiful mess—that's what my family is. And I bet that's what your family is too.

There is no such thing as a "perfect crayon-box family." Oh, I know, some Facebook posts and Instagram feeds lead you to believe otherwise; but it's not true. Not every vacation is as perfect as the family photo on the beach. Not everyone's kid wins the spelling bee. Not every eight-year-old is a black belt nor every twelve-year-old the MVP of the soccer tournament. Photographs can be deceptive, because you don't know the backstory. And when you don't know the backstory, you don't know the whole story.

Photographs can be deceptive, because you don't know the backstory. And when you don't know the backstory, you don't know the whole story.

## The Story Behind the Story

One of my wife's dreams was to go to New York City at Christmas time. We saved and, coupled with airline miles and hotel points, were able to make the trip. Our goal on our last night was to snap a family photo alongside the Christmas tree in Rockefeller Plaza. And we did. It's a pretty good shot. The lights from the 75-foot tree are dancing in the background; other surrounding trees are glowing with white lights. Golden flags are flying above us. We're all together. My wife has our five-year-old Ana in her arms and I'm holding our seven-year-old son, Cade. We're all smiling and Cade has his head on my shoulder. If you saw this on Instagram, you might think, "What a perfect, All-American family."

If only you knew. And you're about to.

The day began with a tour on one of the double-decker buses around Manhattan. It's a pretty cool system. You buy an all-day "hop-on/hop-off" pass that enables you to ride around the city, see the sights at your leisure, and catch the next bus when it comes around. We had strolled through Central Park, jumped on the "Big" piano at FAO Schwartz, ridden the indoor ferris wheel in Toys-R-Us in Times Square, and finished savoring hot chocolate near the Empire State building. That's when the wheels came off. Not literally, but they might as well have.

We just happened to be in the city following the police shootings in Ferguson and New York City. Police rushed to barricade streets. We were quickly escorted out of the area, which happened to be the spot where we were supposed to catch our bus. So we walked. Well, not all of us. It was afternoon and the kids were tired, so Camden and I walked 0.7 miles, carrying the kids to the next stop. That's where we waited. And waited, and waited. Even though a call to the bus company assured us the stop was still on the route, the bus never came. One final call told us it had been rerouted. And so we walked again.

We finally made it to the next stop and reboarded the bus. The only problem: the bus was full and the only available seats were in a spot where we were susceptible to the inhalation of the exhaust fumes.

After another two hours of touring, we arrived back at Rockefeller Center and got off the bus still determined to get that family photo. Apparently everyone else in Manhattan had the same idea, because Rockefeller Plaza was packed. I'm talking shoulder-to-shoulder packed. This country boy was getting claustrophobic, but we pressed on. As we made our way through the sea of people towards the tree, I spotted the perfect scenario—a couple was taking a selfie in front of the tree. I quickly realized this was our chance for the reciprocal photo offer. I would offer to take their picture and, in turn, ask them to take ours.

I snapped a few pictures of them with their iPhone and handed them our phone. So there we were. The moment was all arranged: tree lit up in the background, a third-party photographer, our family together. Camden grabbed Ana and I bent down to pick up Cade. But when I lifted him up, I accidentally smacked his knee off of a metal fence post. He immediately burst into tears.

I was not going to have this. We had navigated our way around protests, tracked down buses, and made our way through a sea of hundreds of thousands of people. We were going to get this photo taken and we were going to be smiling if it killed us! So I uttered a line in Cade's ear that will not soon be engraved on any Father-of-the-Year awards. While I'll leave the specific wording out, the gist of my warning: *You are going to stop crying and smile or there will be well, umm, consequences.*

Let me save you the email explaining what a horrible father I was at that moment. I already know. I know it wasn't Cade's fault. I realize I am the one who smacked his knee on a metal pole in cold weather. And I know I reacted out of frustration and anger, and out of desire to get a perfect picture in order to look good in front of other people.

Because we want to look good in front of others, don't we? No matter how much of a mess the crayon box is at home, we want to look to others like the crayon box fresh off the toy store shelf. We can end up parenting for the public, either by threatening, punishing, bribing, or giving in to our kids based not on what's best for them, but on how it makes us appear as parents in front of other people.

Furthermore, we also compare ourselves and our families to things that aren't real. We see snapshots of other families' lives and make comparisons based on the illusory images. Nobody posts a picture of his or her kid after he or she just lost the spelling bee. We don't see many tweets about someone's child after she just gave up the game-winning goal. Few people jump on Facebook right after their kid got pinned in the first 20 seconds of the wrestling match. And the snapshots we do see aren't the whole story. What might seem like a smiling picture in front of a Christmas tree can sometimes hide a backstory of extreme weariness, frustration, and failure.

---

We can end up comparing ourselves and our families to things that aren't real.

---

Again, it goes back to our key scripture,

> *"The LORD does not look at the things people look at. People look at the outward appearance, but the LORD looks at the heart."*

It's so easy to be consumed with outward appearances. I want to look good. I want my kids to look good. So it can be easy to parent toward that end. But what's important to us isn't always the thing that's important to God. And what's important to God isn't always the thing that is important to us.

The myth of the perfect crayon box family is just the beginning, and the pictures on social media are the result of something deeper.

The underlying modern-day philosophy of parenting is loaded with destructive myths. In this chapter, we will uncover and expose some of these popular parenting myths.

Before we dive into these myths, be advised that we're going under the knife. If I go to the doctor's office for any reason, I like plenty of explanation. If the doctor barges in and starts poking and prodding without explanation, I get agitated. But if he or she explains what will happen, and how it will benefit me, I have a different attitude. So allow me to explain a few things. First, I'm not a hater. While we're going to examine our culture of youth sports, it's not because I don't like sports. On the contrary, I probably like them too much. Some of my best childhood memories are of playing baseball. My son plays baseball and soccer. And we're committed Pittsburgh sports fans complete with Terrible Towels and Pirate hats.

Second, going under the scalpel is, often times, uncomfortable. Yet the final goal is not pain, but health. Some of what we're going to uncover will be hard to read. At least it was hard for me to write, as I looked in the mirror and recognized some of these patterns in myself. Hang in there, because God only guides us into spiritual heart surgery for the purpose healing and freedom.

Finally, while the following predominantly focuses on youth sports, it has as much application to the arts and academics. It doesn't matter if it's baseball or ballet, or if your kid is an athlete or mathlete, the principles remain true.

**MYTH #1: The earlier I get my child involved in an activity, the greater their skill set in that area will be and the better chance they will have at succeeding long-term.**

**TRUTH: There is no research that supports this theory. It is actually a modern development with no backing.**

The focus of stage parenting is rooted in the basic belief that success in life depends on the development of talents and abilities. This theory is founded upon something called the cognitive hypothesis. The cognitive hypothesis states that "success depends primarily on the development of a skill set, and that the best way to develop that skill is to practice as much as possible, beginning as early as possible."[1] This theory has become so pervasive that economists from the University of California refer to the increased competition among parents for early academic achievement as the "Rug Rat Race."

The Rug Rat Race is rampant in modern parenting. "If my son is going to succeed in soccer, I better get him in the best league with the best coach and on as many traveling teams as possible, as young as possible." "If my daughter is going to be a singer, I better get her the best voice coach and on stage as young as possible." "If my child is going to get into the best college, I better get him or her into the best preschool."

Because the cognitive hypothesis is so widespread and has become such a mainstay of modern-day parenting culture, perhaps we don't realize it's a fairly new theory. It didn't come onto the scene until 1994. That alone should cause skepticism. You mean to tell me that prior to 1994, kids didn't succeed? You mean we've been parenting wrongly for thousands of years and it's only in the past two decades we've discovered the real secrets of raising successful kids?

The second problem is even more profound. Because of its newness, there has been little research investigating the critical question: Does it work? But the research has begun, especially with the first generation of kids raised under this parenting philosophy emerging into adulthood. Educational researchers are beginning to gather data on the Rug Rat Race Generation. The conclusion is: "Oops! We were wrong!" Researcher and author Paul Tough has written a magnificent *New York Times* bestseller exposing the lies of the Rug

Rat Race entitled *How Children Succeed*. He writes, "The conventional wisdom about child development over the past few decades has been misguided. We have been focusing on the wrong skills and abilities in our children, and we have been using the wrong strategies to help nurture and teach those skills."[2] Tough concludes that it's not test scores, talent, or travel leagues that contribute to a child's future success, but rather grit, curiosity, and character.

Brussels University in Belgium recently performed a study determining whether performances at a young age are a good predictor of later success.[3] The conclusion: No, not really. They studied several different sports; we will take tennis as an example. Researchers found that successful performance at age 14 is not necessary for later success, and good performances in youth tournaments are no guarantee of success at higher levels. The study went on to show that correlations between current and future success don't show up in girls until fifteen and boys until seventeen.[4] According to their studies, there was no evidence that getting children involved with great leagues, teams, or instructors at an early age connects to their long-term success.

---

There's no evidence that getting children involved with great leagues, teams, or instructors at an early age connects to their long-term success.

---

Bob Bigelow, a former first-round NBA draft pick and current professional NBA scout, agrees. These days Bigelow travels the country lecturing about what is wrong with youth sports in America. He has written a must-read book for any parent or coach, *Just Let the Kids Play: How to Stop Other Adults from Ruining Your Child's Fun and Success in Youth Sports*. Bob refers to most youth sports leagues and especially elite travel teams as "perhaps the most destructive force in youth sports today," and rails against "the misguided efforts by adults to identify and cultivate sports 'talent' at a younger and younger age."[5] He goes on to say that "I have no doubt that players today are *no better* than players of previous generations. In fact, some things, such as teamwork, have suffered."[6] Keep in mind, this assessment isn't coming from a disgruntled parent whose kid did didn't make the cut. This is coming from an NBA scout.

Dean Conway, head state coach of the Massachusetts Youth Soccer Association asks the question, "Where is the best soccer in the world at the youth level being played right now?" His answer: certainly not at the youth rec centers in the U.S. with all-star teams and manicured fields, and loads of coaches and parents dictating every move. It's being played in the dusty streets of South America and Europe. And it's from these carefree environments devoid of adult intervention that some of the best soccer players in the world emerge.[7]

Ditto for baseball. Out of the unorganized, kids-playing-in-the streets environment of the Dominican Republic emerge some of baseball's brightest stars. Keith Lippman, director of player development for the Oakland Athletics says, "less instruction is better at younger levels. That's why a lot of times the Dominicans are easier to work with. They haven't had a lot of instruction." He goes on to compare these "live athletes" with the kids coming out of the U.S. system. He says, "Then you see our kids and they are so thick and slow at eighteen that they are already cooked. You don't see active, live bodies."[8]

But you know this already, don't you? You know it instinctively. Remember that thing called puberty? You know that kids' bodies, minds, and desires change drastically in the middle-school years. Just because a kid was (or wasn't) great at something in first, fourth, or seventh grade doesn't mean that he or she will (or won't) be great at the same thing later in life. (Now would be a good time to remember the clumsy kid in your elementary school who ended up being a fabulous athlete in high school.)

Think of how crazy this is, especially because recent estimates say that approximately 70% of kids quit sports by the time they are in middle school. When asked why they give up, a number of kids point to the adults in charge who suck the fun out of the sport.[9] How many of these burnt out kids hadn't even begun to outgrow their "clumsy" phase? And how many of the "top" kids simply hit a growth spurt sooner than everyone else?

When asked by parents what advice he would give them, six-time NBA champion Michael Jordan says, "Let [your kids] just enjoy the game. ...Once they learn a love for the game at a young age, the developmental part is easy." Jordan continues, "I didn't really get instruction until I was a junior in high school. Play early, but learn late."[10] For Jordan, a love of the game was developed on the playgrounds of his hometown in Wilmington, NC or on one-on-one battles in his backyard with his brother. The greatest player in the game didn't learn on a travel team; he learned on playgrounds and backyards.

---

> "I didn't get instruction until I was a junior in high school. Play early, but learn late." –Michael Jordan.

---

This should give you great freedom as a parent, because this choice is not a matter of sacrificing your child's future. This is not: "Well, I guess if I choose not to push my child at an early age, they won't have an opportunity to succeed, but it's best for them so oh well." This approach is not an either/or; this is a both/and. You can choose to protect the ecosystem of childhood *and* have your child excel. If your child is going to excel in baseball in high school and beyond, the best thing you can do is keep it innocent and playful during elementary school. If your daughter is going to excel in the arts at sixteen, the best thing you can do is not to push her at six. What a shame for the world to be filled with dancers who no longer like to dance.

---

This approach is a both/and. You can choose to protect the ecosystem of childhood *and* have your child excel.

---

**MYTH #2: Travel teams, private instructors, and elite competitions are a good financial investment in my child's future.**

**TRUTH: Your money feeds the machine.**

You don't need to rubber neck too much while driving to see the plethora of minivans and SUV's plastered with stickers, magnets, and writing on the windows advertising their child's involvement in travel sports teams and dance competitions. Have you walked into Dick's Sporting goods lately and seen the youth sports section? It has become a machine.[11]

Take a guess at what is the fastest growing segment in the travel industry. Vacations? That would be nice, but no. Business? Based on the number of people I encounter on a regular basis in the Atlanta airport, it's doing fine, but that's not it either. According to Dave Hollander, professor at New York University's Tisch Center for Hospitality, the fastest growing segment in travel is youth sports. "Youth sports tourism wasn't even a category four years ago," Hollander says, "and now it's the fastest-growing segment in travel. You've got millions of kids involved, parents spending thousands of dollars, and cities building facilities to host events and chase tourism dollars," he said. "It's just huge."[12]

According to a CNBC report, children's sports has become a $7 billion a year industry—in travel alone! That amount doesn't include uniforms, equipment, or tournament entry fees. According to a University of Florida Sport Policy and Research report, travel-team parents spend an average of $2266 annually on their child's participation. At some levels, that number can go above $20,000.[13]

Why the tremendous investment in this type of activity at such a young age? It goes back to the cognitive hypothesis and the hope that it will pay dividends pertaining to the child's success in these areas. But will it? Let's look at the numbers.

I remember when I played Little League, it was a big deal what number I wore. I usually wanted to pick the number of one of my favorite Major League players. For instance, when I played T-Ball, I wanted to be number 5, the number worn by the great-hitting Pittsburgh Pirates third baseman Bill "Mad Dog" Matlock. But perhaps in today's leagues it would be best to give each child the same number: 0.01. That's the statistical probability of a Little Leaguer making it to the Major Leagues. Actually, it's less than 0.01%. Not 1%. Not even 0.01%. *Less than* 0.01%. Statistically speaking, you have a greater chance of winning the lottery or being struck by lightning ... six times![14]

---

The statistical probability of a Little Leaguer making it to the Major Leagues is less than 0.01%. Statistically speaking, you have a greater chance of winning the lottery or being struck my lightening ... six times!

---

The statistics from other sports are similar. According to research from the NCAA, the percent of high school athletes who will go pro in various sports is:

Men's Basketball: 0.03%
Women's Basketball: 0.03%
Football: 0.08%
Men's Soccer: 0.09%[15]

Keep in mind these statistics are from *high school* to the pros. The number of kids who, for instance, play youth soccer is now over 3 million (compared to 411,000 who play in high school).[16] If you run those numbers, the percentage of children in your kid's soccer league who will play professionally drops to 0.01%. (But you probably guessed that already.)

*That's the pros,* you might be thinking. *They might at least get a college scholarship.* But the stats on that one are not in your favor either. Only about two percent of high school varsity athletes end up playing Division I sports, let alone getting a scholarship. Oh and by the way, that $2266 the average family spends on travel leagues, if invested in an Educational Savings Account from the time your child is 8-18, would produce $44,798. Can you say "college fund"?[17]

That puts it into perspective, doesn't it? So when your kid misses a ground ball or the ump misses a call, keep all of this in mind. Nobody is paying your kid to play ball now and chances are, they won't in the future. But even if your kids don't take home a paycheck, they will take home memories. By focusing on meaningful time together and positive, fun memories, you win every time.

**MYTH #3: Lots of organized activities are good character development and will help my child in whatever field he or she chooses.**

**TRUTH: Over-involvement in childhood activities takes a toll on a child, both emotionally and physically.**

## Emotional Stress

Ask almost any parent or coach what the number one benefit of youth athletics is and you are liable to get the same answer: "It builds character." But does it? Does submitting our children to high-pressure, high-stress situations on the stage and under the spotlight really build character? Or does it lead somewhere else?

Dr. Burke Harris is a Harvard-educated physician and lead pediatrician of the Bayview Childhood Health Center in the southeast corner of San Francisco. Dr. Harris sought to make headway in the area of childhood health and found herself increasingly frustrated at the lack of results. She set out to find answers. In doing so, she came across a medical journal article entitled, "The Relationship of Adverse Childhood Experiences to Adult Health." When Harris read the article, something clicked.

The study represented a very mainstream group—mostly white, middle to upper class individuals. Seventy-five percent were white and college educated. The questionnaire to this group asked them to rate their childhood experiences in ten different negative categories including physical and sexual abuse, neglect, divorce or separation, and living in an environment where an adult was addicted to drugs or alcohol. When the results of the study were collected, common sense would indeed suggest some correlation between negative experiences during childhood and adult health problems. But it wasn't just a casual connection. The correlation between Adverse Childhood Conditions (referred to as an "ACE" score) and negative health as adults were so strong that it "stunned" the researchers.

The study noted that "compared to people with no history of ACE's, people with ACE scores of 4 or higher were twice as likely to smoke, seven times more likely to be alcoholics, and seven times more likely to have had sex before fifteen. They were twice as likely to have been diagnosed with cancer, twice as likely to have heart disease, twice as likely to have liver disease, four times as likely to suffer from emphysema or chronic bronchitis. ...Adults with an ACE score above 6 were thirty times more likely to have attempted suicide than those with an ACE score of 0. And men with an ACE score above 5 were forty-six times more likely to have injected drugs than men with no history of ACE's."[18]

While the degree of correlation may be surprisingly high, the correlation itself at least makes sense. Children who have been sexually abused seem more likely to engage in sexual activity at an earlier age. Children of alcoholics seem more likely to drink excessively themselves. But the twist Burke discovered in the research was just as shocking. The underlying common denominator in these situations that correlated to high ACE scores was not necessarily the negative experiences in and of themselves, it was the *stress* related to those experiences.

To understand this correlation, it's helpful to understand how our bodies process stress. The body is designed to regulate stress with a system called the HPA (hypothalamic-pituitary-adrenal) axis. You experience this with "fight or flight" reactions that come from being in contact with immediate danger. If you walk around a street corner at night and encounter a guy with a gun, the HPA axis goes into hyper-drive. Gun. Adrenaline rush. Swing your fist or run fast. Back to normal. But most of us don't live with gun encounters as a regular occurrence. The stress produced in most of our lives is not usually physical, but mental, such as worrying about a relationship, mortgage, job, or finances. The problem is that the HPA axis is not designed to handle ongoing stress. Its purpose is to deal with "fight or flight" responses quickly, flush them out, and be done. But worry and anxiety don't work like that. The "toxins" produced by this kind of stress don't get filtered out. Rather, they overflow into our bodies causing all kinds of long-term health consequences.

This is especially true in children. In his entertaining and insightful book, *Why Zebra's Don't Get Ulcers,* Neuroscientist Robert Sapolsky writes, "Overloading the HPA axis, especially in infancy and childhood, produces all kinds of serious and long-lasting negative effects—physical, psychological, and neurological."[19] If a zebra is grazing beside a peaceful watering hole and suddenly a lion attacks, its stress levels go through the roof. But in this "fight or flight" moment (for the zebra, its always "flight"!) the zebra takes off running. After the episode is over, the stress is over. Like the zebra, our bodies are designed to incur physical stress for a brief amount of time, not emotional stress for an elongated amount of time.

## Inside Out & Stress Island

Now connect this understanding of stress with the power of childhood memories, as shown in Disney Pixar's film, *Inside Out.* In this movie, we see inside eleven-year-old Riley's brain and get a behind-the-scenes tour of how emotions like joy, sadness, anger, fear, and disgust play out at the "control center". While many of Riley's childhood memories are forgotten (such as her imaginary part cotton-candy, part elephant, part dolphin, part cat friend, Bing-Bong), and others seem to pop into her head randomly (the tune from an old chewing-gum commercial), there are other key memories that are called "core memories." These core memories form islands, such as Friendship Island, Goofball Island, and Family Island, which in turn become the building blocks of Riley's personality.

Beyond being highly entertaining, the film is extremely accurate in its portrayal of how emotion, memory, and personality are formed. In an article for *Psychology Today*, Janina Scarlet writes, "What's really powerful about this film is how accurate it is to cognitive, developmental, and clinical psychology."[20] Core memories form islands, which become the building blocks of personality.

Now let's connect the dots. What Burke's research shows is that children raised in environments of continual stress form "stress islands" which have a profound negative effect throughout their lives. We see today a staggering number of teenagers who are suffering from severe anxiety and panic attacks. This begs the question: what is the high-pressure, high-competition world of childhood athletics, academics, and arts doing to our kids?

> Children raised in environments of continual stress form "stress islands" which have a profound negative effect throughout their lives. This begs the question: what is the high-pressure, high-competition world of athletics, academics, and arts doing to our kids?

## Physical Stress

We've talked about the emotional and mental toll that this "too much too soon" lifestyle can have on kids. But it's also physical. "Lyle Micheli, the youth sports medicine pioneer, estimates that of the seventy young patients who file into his clinic each Thursday at Children's Hospital Boston, 75 percent are victims of overuse injuries."[21] When I was growing up, it was pitchers at the end of their careers who had Tommy John surgery. Now it's common for players to have it in their early twenties, sometimes even before they break into the major leagues. I recently heard the story of a retired NFL player who, at age 36, is having trouble climbing stairs and regrets playing football because of the physical toll it has taken on his body. It's time to seriously consider the effects that travel teams and year-round activities are having on our kids. A middle school kid shouldn't be entering sixth grade mentally burnt out, emotionally stressed out, and physically worn out.

On the contrary, if you allow your child to have just limited involvement with activities during elementary school, think of the potential advantage you will give them. While other kids are worn out, burnt out, and stressed out, it will be the children who were allowed to have a childhood who will enter middle school full of energy and confidence.

---

While other kids are worn out, burnt out, and stressed out, it will be the children who were allowed to have a childhood who will enter middle school full of energy and confidence.

---

**MYTH #4: This is about my child.**

**TRUTH: Is it?**

I was listening to Andy Stanley's podcast on parenting when the host asked a great question, "When you are rooting for your kid, are you rooting for the name on the front of the jersey, or the back?" In other words, who are you really rooting for? The team? Or the family name? Who's this really about? Psychologists call it "achievement by proxy syndrome"—parents who glean their sense of self-worth from their daughter getting the lead in the school play or their son being the star of the basketball team.

Chap Clark is among the who's who of experts on childhood, adolescence, and parenting, and serves as the professor of youth, family, and culture at Fuller Theological Seminary. He's a popular author, conference speaker, and brings more than 30 years of practical ministry experience into his work. Chap's latest book, *Hurt 2.0,* is a first-hand report on the results of the Rug Rat Race.

In conducting research for his book, Clark didn't just study piles of data; he lived among students. Clark took a year to serve as a substitute high school teacher. He wanted to observe students in their environment first-hand: to watch them, talk to them, and hear their stories. As a sub, he would spend the first part of the class teaching, then would put the materials away and explain why he was really there. He was writing a book and wanted to hear their stories. As you can imagine, students were at first a bit skeptical and hesitant, but as he developed relationships and earned their trust, the students opened up.

One of the things he discovered was both fascinating and heartbreaking. Many students described having a "wake-up" experience as they entered adolescence. It went something like this: "I came to the realization that my childhood wasn't really a childhood. All of those soccer games and baseball tournaments, talent competitions and gifted academic programs—they weren't about me. They were about my parents. I was just a pawn in my parent's dreams." As students came to this realization, they experienced profound disillusionment. They went searching for reality and meaning in other areas.[22] Clark concludes, "These activities are no longer for or about the students; they are for and about the adults in charge."[23]

Brilliant child psychologist turned family-life educator, Dr. Wendy Mogul agrees. She says, "I've come to believe that many of the problems in the children I've counseled arose from two sources: the heavy pressure in a competitive world and their unconscious recognition of how preternaturally important they were to their parents."[24]

---

> "I've come to believe that many of the problems in the children I've counseled arose from two sources: the heavy pressure in a competitive world and their unconscious recognition of how preternaturally important they were to their parents."
> –Dr. Wendy Mogul

---

For parents, we should remember that the end goal isn't raising a great eight-year-old, but rather a competent, healthy, and independent eighteen-year-old. When we're caught up in the moment, flying the plane back up to 30,000 feet and seeing the big picture can be helpful.

When my kid is eighteen and leaving the house for college, what do I want him or her to remember from childhood? For instance, I love what my good friend continually reminds his own kids about baseball: "This is about fun and memories."

---

The goal of parenting isn't to raise a great eight-year-old, but a competent, healthy, and independent eighteen-year-old.

---

**MYTH #5: Jesus is happy with the parenting systems in America.**

**TRUTH: Let's explore scripture.**

Remember felt boards in Sunday School class? One thing I remember about the characters on those boards is that Jesus always seemed to be smiling. Whether he was providing food for thousands, carrying a lamb, or healing a blind man, felt-board Jesus always had a smile on his face. I think that most of the time that portrayal is pretty accurate. But not always. In fact, there are times when Jesus got mad. Really mad.

One of those instances had to do with how children were being treated. Against the backdrop of the disciples arguing among themselves about who would be the greatest in the kingdom of heaven, Jesus brings in a child and replies, "Truly I tell you, unless you change and become like little children, you will never enter the kingdom of heaven. Therefore, whoever takes the lowly position of this child is the greatest in the kingdom of heaven. And whoever welcomes one such child in my name welcomes me."[25]

And just in case the "importance of children" theme isn't clear, Jesus continues,

> If anyone causes one of these little ones—those who believe in me—to stumble, it would be better for them to have a large millstone hung around their neck and to be drowned in the depths of the sea. Woe to the world because of the things that cause people to stumble! Such things must come, but woe to the person through whom they come! If your hand or your foot causes you to stumble, cut it off and throw it away. It is better for you to enter life maimed or crippled than to have two hands or two feet and be thrown into eternal fire. And if your eye causes you to stumble, gouge it out and throw it away. It is better for you to enter life with one eye than to have two eyes and be thrown into the fire of hell.[26]

Whoa! Hold on. I don't remember felt-board Jesus reacting like with such force! But the real Jesus did. These are tough words. Hard words. But they are real words. One thing that took a smile off the face of Jesus was anything that took smiles off the faces of children.

One thing that took a smile off the face of Jesus was anything that took smiles off the faces of children.

What does that mean for us today? We are rightly horrified by any person or system that exploits children. We are enraged when we hear of a child being exploited sexually to fulfill the twisted desires of the abuser. We cringe when we hear of children in sweatshops being exploited to fulfill corporate greed. But what about middle-class success-culture exploitation? What about taking our children and putting them on stages and sports fields to fulfill our own needs? *Come on, Doug, that's an extreme metaphor!* But is it? The heart of any type of child exploitation is an adult using a child to fulfill his or her own needs.

A recent film shows children dressed up and catered to, given the finest food and clothing.[27] They are trained by the best mentors; they are brought on stage to the cheers of adoring masses; they become the pride of their hometowns. What a wonderful life, or so it would seem. The only problem is they're trained to fight each other ... to the death. Perhaps *Hunger Games* provides a metaphor for the western world's "celebrification" of our children—even if it causes their destruction.

After reading this, you might assume that I hate Little League and all organized activities. Please let me remind you: I don't. Some of my fondest memories are of playing ball as a kid. Our son plays sports. What I am raising a red flag against is "too much, too soon." It's not good for your family. It's not good for your child.

"Dylan" was a kid on my son's baseball team when I served as assistant coach. He was a smiling, fun-loving boy, and a good athlete. By the time the next season rolled around, I was excited to see he was on our team again. But this time was different. He had spent the summer on a travel team, and his parents had hired a private instructor to work with him. They had also put him on medication for ADHD, which he may or may not have had needed. I hardly ever saw Dylan smile that season. He didn't seem to enjoy himself at all, looking more like a kid being force-fed broccoli and sent to the salt mines than a boy playing a game. He was six years old.

## Time to Take Down the Giant

When David was a boy, Goliath came out every day to taunt the Israelites. He beat down an entire nation of warriors with fear and intimidation. Nobody had the courage to stand up to this giant until one young boy emerged from a shepherd's field and said, "This is ridiculous. Why are we living our lives like this?" So with a confidence that God would win the battle, he took his sling and a stone and defeated the giant.

The "giant" of competition taunts today's parents with fear and intimidation. "Your kid is falling behind. You need to get him or her involved in more activities. Look at what everyone else is doing." Enough is enough. We've been bullied long enough with fear tactics from a giant seeking to intimidate the people of God into parenting according to misguided values. It's time to stand up to Goliath. It's time to unleash the stone.

We've been bullied long enough with fear tactics from a giant seeking to intimidate the people of God into parenting according to misguided values. It's time to stand up to Goliath.

Are you ready? Ask yourself these questions: Are my children involved in too many activities? Are my children too young to be in organized activities? Are we too rushed and busy as a family? Are we getting enough family time at home? Are my kids at risk for getting burnt out? Am I parenting to please God or out of pressure to keep up with other people's kids? Am I being true to myself, to my family, and to what is best for them? In my gut, do I feel like something is "off"? Will I shrink back in fear and parent like other people? Or, like David, will I be willing to step out in faith and courage to do something about it?

At first, these decisions will be tough. The challenge not to compare, not to push, not to want to jump full force into the rug rat race for fear of falling behind, can be a great pressure indeed. Even after reading studies from experts stating that elite programs don't give kids a competitive advantage, it can be hard to release the stone. But once you do, watch the giant fall, watch the giant of anxiety in your life fall, and watch the giant of stress in your family fall.

Here's my hunch. I bet there are loads of parents who feel the way you do. Our kids started to show interest in something; so, wanting to be good, supportive parents, we signed them up for activities or leagues. But once it began, something didn't feel right. We saw adults behaving in ways that were questionable at best and awful at worst. We wondered if ours kids were truly having fun, and we started seeing emotions and actions in ourselves that we didn't like. But what do we do now? Is this just the way it is? Do we have to play by these rules if we want our kids to succeed?

We just exposed the fact that the emperor isn't wearing any clothes. Now the choice is up to us. A million Israelites wanted to be free from the tyranny of the Philistines. One had the courage to pick up a sling. I'm calling out the David parents. I'm summoning the holy rebels. Once Goliath fell, hundreds of thousands danced and sang in victory. My guess is that it will only take a few brave parents willing to stand up to the giant that will free others to follow.

## #OPTOUT

As I write, the days of Thanksgiving are approaching which naturally brings the beginning of the holiday shopping season with its kickoff on Black Friday. But while stores used to open at 5AM on Friday morning, stores are now opening at midnight, and even on Thanksgiving Day.

Outdoor outfitter REI captured the hearts of millions by saying "Enough!" The retail giant decided to close all of its 143 stores on Black Friday, pay all of its employees, and lead a movement to #OptOutside. The company won't even process web orders until the following day and has launched a website with links to nearby hiking trails and places for users to "explore the outdoors."

A marketing campaign? Sure. But a powerful one that has struck a chord in the hearts of millions. Parents, it's a good message for us as well. It's time to #OptOut. It's time to boldly say "No" to the rug rat race that's destroying our families. What began as an extra-curricular activity here and there has turned into an all-invasive force on our family's time and budget. Just as Black Friday should not invade Thanksgiving, we should stop allowing extra-curricular activities to overtake and overwhelm our families. Enough is enough.

In a "stage parenting" culture, God is still looking for children with a heart like David's. The Lord is again looking for a generation of champions. He's looking for giant killers and world changers. He's looking for young men and women to anoint for greatness. But, surprise, He's not looking where we think. He's not looking on the stage of the public arena. He's looking in the hiddenness and obscurity of the field.

## Group Discussion Guide

1) Briefly revisit each of the five parenting myths. Which of the myths do you most likely identify? Which do you least identify with in your parenting style? Why or why not?
2) Why do you think these myths so widely appeal to parents?
3) What steps are you willing to take in order to change the pressure placed upon your child(ren) to succeed? How far are you willing to go in order to turn your identifiable myth into truth?
4) If you chose to "Opt Out" what would that look like for you and your family? Take a look at your family calendar. How much "family" time is spent at events for your children? What activities could you put on the "Opt Out" list? What could life for you, your family, and your children look like on the other side of "Opting Out?"

# 3

## A Child Who Loves Jesus

*"I have found David son of Jesse, a man after my own heart."*

*(Acts 13:22)*

As parents, we enjoy hearing people say complimentary things about our kids. I remember times when my children were babies, and I would run an errand. Sometimes I would take my kids with me for selfish reasons—I wanted to show them off. I know it sounds pretty self-serving, but I liked hearing sweet old ladies in the checkout line at the grocery store make a fuss over my kids. (For some reason the construction dudes at Lowes usually didn't have the same reaction, but oh well.) No matter their age, my heart swells with pride if someone compliments my children.

But as I read the line describing David as "a man after God's own heart," I can't think of anything I'd rather have said about my kids. Not now; not when they're teenagers hanging out with friends after school; not when they're college kids studying for exams; not when they walk down the aisle; not when they launch their careers; not when they're chasing little kids of their own; or not when they're becoming old and grey. I can't think of anything better—ever. If Cade and Ana are described by the Lord as "a man and woman after my own heart," that's truly the best I could want for them. I bet you would say the same about your kids.

So, moms and dads, how do we accomplish this goal? It sure seems like a pretty daunting task. I know it does for me. Sometimes I can't get my kids to sit still during a five-minute family devotion on the couch. How am I going to raise them to be champions for Jesus if we can't read through Moses and the burning bush without a fight? The only thing I know is to go back to scripture for guidance.

## A Man After God's Own Heart

God says a lot of good things about a lot of people in the Bible. Despite all their weaknesses, flaws, and failures, Moses was humble, Peter was a rock, Noah was righteous, and Mary was highly favored. But perhaps one of the all-time greatest statements the Lord made about any individual other than Jesus are the words spoken about David when he is described as a man after God's own heart:

> *But the Lord said to Samuel, "Don't judge by his appearance or height, for I have rejected him. The Lord doesn't see things the way you see them. People judge by the outward appearance, but the Lord looks at the heart" (1 Samuel 16:7, NLT).*

Later in the New Testament, Luke reflects on the same account:

> *After removing Saul, he made David their king. God testified concerning him: "I have found David son of Jesse, a man after my own heart; he will do everything I want him to do" (Acts 13:22).*

Parents, let's not rush past this concept. These scriptures contain a key for success:

God chose David not because of his skill set, but because of his heart.

Unleashing your child's destiny has to do first and foremost not with forming a skill set after man, but cultivating a heart after God. That approach is the exact opposite of how you are being told by society to parent your child. Culture would tell you to focus on developing your child's skill set. But, surprise! God's ways are different than the world's ways. When you have God's heart, the rest flows from there. David had anointing, courage, favor, success, riches, and fame. But all these qualities originated with his heart. Everything always begins with the heart.

---

Unleashing your child's destiny has to do first and foremost not with forming a skill set after man, but cultivating a heart after God.

---

## Heartbeats In Sync

A fascinating study was conducted at the University of Gothenburg in Sweden by professional singer/songwriter-turned-neuroscientist, Bjorn Vickhoff. In his study, Vickhoff investigated whether there was scientific research to back up the sense that people who sing together sometimes have a feeling of connection to one another.

Vickoff assembled a group of fifteen eighteen-year-old students. He hooked them up to EKG machines to monitor their heart rates. At first, as you might expect, each of their heartbeats registered a different rate—some faster and some slower. Then, he had them sing together as a choir. When he did, an amazing thing occurred. Each of their heartbeats came into alignment; as they sang together, their hearts began to beat together.

Here's the science behind the strange phenomenon: your heartbeat is connected to your breathing. The medical term is *respiratory sinus arrhythmia*, or RSA. RSA has been shown to have positive calming effects on the body. For instance, breathing exercises done during yoga have been shown to help with high blood pressure.

A good musician or choral director understands this principle, because when you sing together, you breathe together. Since your breathing is connected to your heartbeat, as you breathe together, your hearts beat together.[1]

Just as we have a heartbeat, so there is a heartbeat from heaven. The Father's heart beats with love, compassion, purpose, and destiny for his children. As we live a life of worship, our heartbeat begins to come into alignment with the heartbeat of heaven. Young David did this perhaps better than any other person on the planet. Somehow in that shepherd's field, he cultivated a life that aligned with the heartbeat of the Father. Thus, the Lord later saying, "That's a kid after my own heart. I choose him."

The ecosystem where this heartbeat developed is crucial to our understanding of David. It was a shepherd's field—a hidden, obscure, off-the-stage and out-of-the spotlight shepherd's field. People didn't know about David. People weren't lining up to give him awards or choose him for their team. And God knew that the best environment for developing a heartbeat in sync with the divine heartbeat is away from the crowds.

---

The best environment for developing a heartbeat in sync with the divine heartbeat is away from the crowds.

---

God still does his best parenting in fields. He develops the heart in the field. God wants to cultivate your child's heart to beat in alignment with his. A song from heaven is being sung over your little boy or little girl. It's a song of purpose and destiny. It's a song of beauty and love. It's a song of faith and a future. God's desire is to cultivate the hearts of his sons and daughters to beat in alignment with his heart. This process can't be rushed. If it's short-circuited, the child emerges with a heart defect.

What could be better as a parent than your child's heart beating in alignment with the heartbeat of his or her Heavenly Father? This alignment is God's desire for your children. He wants our kids to live a life of worship, which is a life in tune with the song of heaven, breathing with the breath of the Father, with a heartbeat aligned with His heart.

*When you sing together, you breathe together.*
*When you breathe together, your hearts beat together.*

## THAT'S GREAT... BUT HOW?

Most parents would agree that having their children cultivate God's own heart would be a win in the parenting department. The problem is, how? I mean, other than selling your home, buying a shepherd's field, throwing a robe around your kid, and shoving a staff in his or her hands, how do you accomplish this? What does this look like in a twenty-first century home? It's a great question. Remember, the key is *environment*. We want to place our children in environments that are most conducive to their heartbeats coming into alignment with the heartbeat of the Father.

Recently, The National Study for Youth and Religion embarked on a research project that attempted to identify factors in the ecosystem in childhood and adolescence that contributed to students serving Jesus as adults. Four of the chief factors were:

1) Connection to the parent or spiritual parent (The Family)
2) Involvement in discipleship (The Church)
3) Involvement in ministry (Ministry)
4) Spiritual benchmark moments (Benchmark Events)

Or, in other words, to receive proper spiritual nourishment, every child needs four different tables in his or her life: the kitchen table (the family), the Lord's table (the church), serving at the table (ministry), and the Thanksgiving table (benchmark events). Let's investigate these areas in greater depth.

## THE KITCHEN TABLE (THE FAMILY)

For better or worse, the number one factor contributing to your kids serving Jesus as adults is the person holding this book right now. That's right, moms and dads, it's you. Gulp. That may cause you to begin thinking, *I know we should be having family devotions more frequently...* But I'm not going down that road.

I'm not against family devotions. They're probably very good. And I suppose that our family should have them more often. But to be honest, our family devotional times are very scattered. I've tried. And I communicate God's Word for a living! I have a lot of weaknesses, but I'm pretty decent at preaching, teaching, or sharing a devotional thought, except when it comes to my own kids. Apparently I'm horrible at that. Early on, our attempts at family devotional time would result in boredom at best, or an all-out fight at worst. The kids would squirm and fidget. They would argue about who got to sit where. They would argue about who got to answer the Bible trivia question. I think we were *less* close to Jesus at the end of family devotions than we were before we got started!

Maybe you're way better than I am, and the family devotion thing works for you. If it does, awesome. But at the current age of my kids, it doesn't for us. This statement may sound particularly unspiritual coming from a pastor: I've all but given up on family devotions. But I haven't given up on the family altar. It's just taken on a different, well, flavor.

I love what author and psychologist Dr. Wendy Mogel says. She writes that "one traditional Jewish expression for *home* is the same word for a house of worship: *mikdash me'at,* or 'little holy place.'" She goes on to say, "Our dining table with our children is an altar. It has the potential to be the holiest place on the planet."

---

"Our dining table with our children is an altar. It has the potential to be the holiest place on the planet." —Dr. Wendy Mogul.

---

There's a lot of support for the dining table's place of importance in your child's life. As author Leonard Sweet writes in *From Tablet to Table:*

- The #1 factor for parents raising kids who are drug-free, healthy, intelligent, kind human beings? "Frequent family dinners."

- The #1 shaper of vocabulary in younger children, even more than any other family event? "Frequent family dinners."
- The #1 predictor of future academic success for elementary-age children? "Frequent family dinners."
- One of the best safeguards against childhood obesity? "Eating meals together."
- The best prescription to prevent eating disorders among adolescent girls? "Frequent family dinners" that exude a "positive atmosphere."
- The variable most associated with lower incidence of depressive and suicidal thoughts among eleven to eighteen-year-olds? "Frequent family dinners."[2]

Which begs the question, how many times have you been to the family altar this week?

The trend in parenting is to go big, to make everything special—huge family vacations, birthday parties that cost way too much, and lots of restaurants. The problem is that when everything is special, nothing is. Our kids don't need more Disney World and Chuck E. Cheese moments. They need more backyard and kitchen table moments.

---

The problem is that when everything is special, nothing is.

---

I bet you remember the smell of your grandmother's kitchen more than you remember the smell of even your favorite restaurant. I bet you have fonder memories of times in your backyard than you do of times at Chuck E. Cheese. It's time to embrace simple again. It's time to embrace the home again. It's time to raise our children in kitchens and backyards again.

---

It's time to embrace simple again. It's time to embrace the home again. It's time to raise our children in kitchens and backyards again.

---

The trend in parenting is to be busy. We cram our schedules so full of activities—soccer practices, dance lessons, and karate tournaments, because it's all about the kids, right? But the very things we are doing for our kids are robbing the most from our kids.

The trend in parenting is to go digital. The "television as babysitter" is being replaced by "phones and tablet computers as babysitters." Good food and good conversation is becoming quick meals and conversations with screens.

The trend in parenting is to do "drop-off discipleship." We drop our child off for piano lessons, so he or she can be taught to play. We drop our child off at school, so he or she can learn to read. Then we take that same mentality into spiritual development, dropping our child off at church and expecting the children's or youth pastor to disciple him or her in one hour a week, forgetting that discipleship begins in the home. It's time to bring our family back to the altar. It's time to bring our family back to the table.

## The Lord's Table (The Church)

The second table that our kids need is the Lord's Table, which is found in the spiritual community of the church. I grew up in a home where going to church wasn't optional. The weather wasn't an excuse. In Northwest Pennsylvania, I remember sliding down portions of a mile-long, winding hill in the Appalachian foothills near our home to get to church. Obstacles weren't an excuse. When the bridge across the Allegheny River was closed for repairs, we would either drive the (very) long way around, or walk across the unfinished steel beams of the bridge to get to our place of worship. A ballgame on a Sunday? You've got to be kidding. We were in church *every* Sunday.

For many families today, that dedication isn't the case. Will Mancini in his article for *Charisma News* writes that of all the challenging church attendance trends, the most disturbing is not that people are going to church less, it's that committed "regular attenders" are going to church less. People who used to go every week are going three times a month. People who used to go three times are now going two.[3] Pastor of Elevation Church, Steven Furtick, recently scolded his congregation, "Some of you woke up this morning and *asked* your kids if they wanted to go to church today."

---

One of the most disturbing trends is not just that people are going to church less, it's that committed "regular attenders" are going to church less.

---

If the primary family altar is the home, the church is a close second. One of the many reasons for this priority is exposing your children to other influential voices in their lives who will help to mold, shape, and disciple them.

Tim and Lisa are parents of three kids at our church—pretty great kids at that. All three have graduated from high school and love Jesus. Reflecting on their childhood, Lisa says that one of her greatest struggles as a mom was the realization that she couldn't be "super mom." She admits that she wanted to be the one to do it all—lead each of her children in the sinner's prayer, speak life and destiny over their lives, and disciple them into their future. But she realized she couldn't do it. She needed others.

In an email to me, Lisa wrote,

> *If there is something I learned about parenting (the hard way) it's that God never intended us to do it alone. I can't tell you how many times when they were 2, 4, and 6 or 10, 12, and 14, I would cry myself to sleep for one reason or another feeling like I had missed the mark with what God entrusted us with. When I didn't have the answer for them or I couldn't promise them a solution to their hurting heart, I felt like I was failing. It wasn't until the middle school and high school years when I realized my children were surrounded with resources and people who loved them almost as much as I did. They were having God moments that didn't always include me, and eventually I understood … that God never intended for me to be the only one He would use to shape, mold and teach my children.*
>
> *The responsibility we have as parents is to determine which [church family] we choose for our kids. In my life that family was an incredible biological family when they were toddlers. My children don't know life without God-fearing aunts, uncles and grandparents. In their middle school/ high school years that family was [their youth ministry]. Joey isn't Joey without [their small-group leaders] Jon and Steve. Andrea isn't Andrea without Paula and Betsy. Alex isn't Alex without Jon and Charles. These are just a few names.*

As a youth pastor for eleven years and someone who's been involved in youth ministry in other ways for eight additional years, I can tell you different versions of Lisa's story over and over again. Parents who consistently chose church involvement for their families come out ahead time and time again.

> Parents who consistently choose church involvement for their families come out ahead time and time again.

## SERVING AT THE TABLE (MINISTRY)

We must be vigilant in making sure that our children don't just grow up expecting to sit at a table and be served. They need to find a table where they can learn to serve others. Take Mikaela, for instance. Mikaela, a high school senior, just completed her first ministry outreach to her public school. She had felt a growing burden for her unsaved friends and decided to do something about it. Mikaela loves to sing, so she rounded up a group of her friends who also love the arts and formed an outreach called Rebel Radio. The idea was a student-led "talent show" of sorts whereby she and others would share music, poetry, and other artistic expressions. The evening would end with a presentation of the gospel. At the very first event, one hundred classmates showed up, and eight responded to accept Christ.

Mikaela's story with this amazing outreach goes all the way back to sixth grade. Mikaela grew up in church, and when it came time to transition from kids' church to middle school ministry, something caught her attention. She heard an announcement to become involved in ministry, and she did. According to Mikaela, that's when her faith in Christ really came alive. As she stepped out and became involved in ministry at her church, her church friends became a church family. Her desire to sing on stage became a desire to see others come to Christ.

I love what my friend Timothy Eldred says. Tim is the founder and president of a ministry called Endeavor, which advocates for young people to put their faith into action to transform the world. Tim says, "Unless youth learn to lead in the church today, they will leave the church tomorrow." Tim calls for pastors to move from Youth Ministry to Youth IN Ministry. (The same could be said of children—from Children's Ministry to Children IN Ministry.) Today's generation of young people doesn't want to sit on the sidelines. They want to be involved. If your kid is going to be committed to an extra-curricular activity, why not ministry?!

---

"Unless youth learn to lead in the church of today, they will leave the church of tomorrow. We must move from youth ministry to youth *in* ministry." —Timothy Eldred

---

## The Thanksgiving Table (Benchmark Events)

Finally, our kids need a Thanksgiving table. Every meal is important. We need to eat every day. But can you imagine a year without a Thanksgiving feast or Christmas dinner? Raising your kids without benchmark spiritual experiences is like going a year without Christmas.

---

Raising your kids without benchmark spiritual experiences is like going a year without Christmas.

---

On my son Cade's eighth birthday, he had a sleepover with two of his cousins, Asher and Soren, and one of his best friends, Keagan. They were sitting at the kitchen table eating pizza, telling stories, and laughing. They were reminiscing and sharing memories like long-lost friends catching up on their childhood. So what was the subject of all of this excitement? Summer Camp.

I've been involved to one degree or another in summer camps for twenty years. I was a counselor at camps during my college years; I took kids to them (and retreats) for eleven years as a youth pastor; and I have been involved in leading statewide camps for the past eight years. Now I am sending my own kids, and I can tell you from two decades of experience that there is a marked difference between kids who go to a Christian summer camp and kids who don't.

*But isn't God the same everywhere? Can't they just have that experience on Sundays at church?*

No. Well, yes, and no. Yes, God is the same everywhere, but no, camp is different than church. There is no replacing a summer camp experience for the development of your child's spiritual life. There is just something about getting away, something about a change of place and a change of pace. There is something about days of summer and sunshine and creating memories. There is something about putting down a tablet computer and picking up a canoe oar. There is something about games and teams and cheers. And there is definitely something about camp altars.

The reason behind this unique environment is what I call a theology of Bethels. The story of Jacob at Bethel provides us with a great theology for summer camp—a theology of encounter. Jacob was traveling and the sun had gone down. He decided to stop for the night to sleep. He lay down and grabbed a rock for a pillow. At this point, he encountered Yahweh in a dream and discovered his destiny. Jacob responded by surrendering all that held him back, building an altar, and committing fully to the Lord. The Bible describes the event by saying, "He met God at Bethel, and there God spoke with us." Simply put, Bethels are places we go to meet God. Bethels don't come to us. We go to Bethel.

As we read about what took place in Jacob's life, we discover that Bethels are:

1) A Place of Revelation (Gen. 28:13; 35:7b)
2) A Place Where You Lay Down All that Holds You Back (Gen. 35:2)
3) A Place of Promise, Calling, and Destiny (Gen. 28:13c-15; 35:11-12)
4) A Place of Name Change and Identity (Gen. 35:10)
5) A Place Where You Build Altars (Gen. 28:18; 35:14)
6) A Place of Giving (Gen. 28:22b; 35:14b)
7) A Place of Commitment (Gen. 28:20-21)

Read over that list again. Slowly. This time I want you to picture your child experiencing all of these dynamics. I'm visualizing my kids experiencing these things as I write, and I'm wiping tears from my eyes in Starbucks as I do. More than anything, I want all of these for my kids.

I want my kids to have a revelation of Almighty God.
I want my kids to lay down all that might hold them back.
I want my kids to know God's promises, calling, and destiny for their lives.
I want my kids to know their identity in Christ.
I want my kids to build altars.
I want my kids to learn to give.
I want my kids to have a lifetime commitment to their Lord and Savior Jesus Christ.

*But what about the price? Camp is expensive.*

You know what's expensive? Not providing Bethel moments for your children. As a parent, I don't "pay" for camp. I invest in my kids. We pay for video games and Christmas presents. We pay for birthday parties and sneakers. We pay for dance lessons and Little League uniforms. But I invest in summer camp, and I'll take the return on that investment any day.

> I don't "pay" for camp. I invest in my kids.

Recently I was privileged to hear from the fifth ranking member of the U.S. House of Representatives, Congressman James Lankford from Oklahoma. Part of Congressman Lankford's fascinating story is that prior to serving in Washington, he ran a youth camp. With 5,000 students attending per week, and with an estimated ten percent of the entire Oklahoma population having been to this camp, it was no ordinary youth camp. We met with the congressman in a small group setting, so after he shared his story, we were able to ask questions.

Because I help run youth camps, I asked him to speak of the importance of camp as it pertains to the spiritual development of the next generation. The Congressman smiled. He said, "You know, it has been my experience that kids come to camp for two reasons. First, they are going to be at a place for an entire week with a large number of people of the opposite sex. Second, they would get on the bus and say something to the effect of, 'I hear people meet God there. I wonder if that's true?'"

It's true.*

## The Breath and the Heart

Meal-times together (family), spiritual community (church), service (ministry), and Bethel experiences (benchmark events) are all practical ways that we can provide ecosystems where our children can cultivate a heart after God and where they can be filled with the breath of God. Those two dynamics—the heart and the breath—are intricately woven together.

Remember the study on the singers? Your heart is connected to your lungs. When you sing together, you breathe together. When you breathe together, your hearts beat together. Having the heart of God begins with having the breath of God.

In the movie *Signs,* Mel Gibson's son has asthma. Cornered in a frightening situation without his inhaler, the son begins to have an asthma attack. Mel Gibson pulls his son close and holds his head on his chest, telling him, "Breathe with me!"

The Father always wants to pull his children close and say, "Breathe with me."

God breathes three times in scriptures. In the creation narrative, God forms man from the dust of the ground. But Adam does not come alive until the *ruach*, the breath of God, fills his nostrils. As God breathes, man is filled with physical life.

In John 3, when Jesus describes to Nicodemus what it means to be spiritually transformed, to be born again, he describes it in the same terms. The Message reads: "Jesus said, 'Unless a person submits to this original creation—the 'wind-hovering-over-the-water' creation, the invisible moving the visible, a baptism into a new life—it's not possible to enter God's kingdom. When you look at a baby, it's just that: a body you can look at and touch. But the person who takes shape within is formed by something you can't see and touch—the Spirit—and becomes a living spirit.'"

The breath of God fills humanity once again, and we are filled with spiritual life.

Later on, Jesus breathes on his disciples and tells them to "receive the Holy Spirit." This promise comes to fulfillment in the Upper

Room as they are filled with the Spirit of the Living God. What was one of the images of the Upper Room? A mighty roaring wind. Breath. God's breath.

When God breathes, we are filled with physical life, spiritual life, and empowered life. What is more natural than breathing? What is more natural than being filled with the breath of God?

God is calling to a generation,

*Sing with me.*
*Breathe with me.*
*Beat in sync with me.*

"A man or woman after God's own heart." Is this possible for your child? Absolutely. But to receive the blessing of David, we can't be divorced from the ecosystem of David. In a culture clamoring for you to get your kid involved in more and more, remember that God still does his best work in the hiddenness and obscurity of the field.

## Group Discussion Guide

The keys to your children having God's own heart involves receiving nourishment from four tables: The Kitchen Table (The Family), The Lord's Table (The Church), Serving at the Table (Ministry), and The Thanksgiving Table (Benchmark Events). Rate your current status in each of these areas (1 to 5) and then list practical ways to implement or improve these areas in your family.

1) The Kitchen Table (The Family)
   How many meals per week do you eat together as a family around the table? What could you do to increase the quantity and/or quality of those times?
2) The Lord's Table (The Church)
   How many times per month does your family attend church? Is it a priority? What obstacles that get in the way could be removed?
3) Serving at the Table (Ministry)
   If your child is old enough, what ministry is he or she involved in? If none, what opportunities are there for him or her to begin serving others?
4) The Thanksgiving Table (Benchmark Events)
   What opportunities does your church provide for benchmark events (camps, retreats, etc.)? How could you better structure your family calendar and budget to make these a priority?

# 4

## A Child Who Walks in Anointing

*Then the Lord said, "Rise and anoint him; this is the one."*
*...From that day on the Spirit of the Lord came powerfully upon David.*

*(1 Samuel 16:12-13)*

Mishya was a junior at Mankato East High School, a public school in Minnesota. Recently, she had given her life to Christ and had become part of the Fine Arts ministry at her youth group, a program that helps students discover, develop, and deploy their talents in the arts. One of the highlights of this ministry involves state wide District Festivals where students compete in drama, music, photography, and other categories for the chance to advance to nationals. In her youth ministry, Mishya discovered her vocal talents and entered her District Festival. Though it was only her first year in Fine Arts, Mishya excelled, advancing in five different categories.

Mishya also ran track at her public school. She had been talking with her friends about the festival, and they had been asking questions about it. One day after track practice, her friends asked her to show them what she was doing in Fine Arts. He did. On a public high school track, with no stage, no lights, and no sound system, Mishya sang. When she finished, she looked up. Two of her friends, who did not have a relationship with Jesus, had tears running down their cheeks. "That was so amazing," they said. "The song was great, but it feels like there's something else going on. We felt something while you were singing." Mishya explained that what they felt was the presence of God, and right there on the track, she shared her experience with Jesus with her friends and led them to Christ.

Raising kids who have talent is one thing, but raising kids who walk in anointing is another thing altogether. One of the best definitions of "anointing" that I have heard is that it is "the mark of God that brings the response of God." Or, said another way, the anointing invites people into what God is doing. When we walk in anointing, we see results. Perhaps now is a good time to ask, what will be the defining mark upon your children? Their school? Their amount of extra-curricular activities? The brand-name of the tag on their shirt? Their grades? Their abilities? Or the anointing of the Almighty God?

Raising kids who have talent is one thing, but raising kids who walk in anointing is another thing altogether.

## David and the Anointing

As we go back to David's story, we soon see the effects of the anointing on his life. As The Lord tapped Samuel on the shoulder and pointed to David, saying, "That's the one, I choose him," he was subsequently anointed. The scripture reads, "So as David stood there among his brothers, Samuel took the flask of olive oil he had brought and anointed David with the oil. And the Spirit of the Lord came powerfully upon David from that day on" (1 Samuel 16:13). The anointing would become the defining mark upon David's life.

---

The anointing would become the defining mark upon David's life.

---

After David was chosen and anointed, you might think he went straight to the top. Perhaps he went off to "King Training Academy" to be taught by the greatest academic and political minds of the time. He didn't. He went back to the shepherd's field. Because even when a child has been chosen and anointed by the Lord, God may not be done with them in the field. The stage will come soon enough. But we must never rush too quickly past the time of hiddenness.

As David goes back to the sheep, we are given a glimpse into what is going on with Saul. In one of the saddest verses in the Bible, the scripture describes what happened to Saul as a result of his disobedience and hardened heart. "Now the Spirit of the Lord had departed from Saul, and an evil spirit from the Lord tormented him" (v. 14). Saul's attendants, recognizing the situation, set out to help the king. They suggested bringing in someone who could play the lyre.

> "See, an evil spirit from God is tormenting you. Let our lord command his servants here to search for someone who can play the lyre. He will play when the evil spirit from God comes on you, and you will feel better." So Saul said to his attendants, "Find someone who plays well and bring him to me." One of the servants answered, "I have seen a son of Jesse of Bethlehem who knows how to play the lyre. He is a brave

> man and a warrior. He speaks well and is a fine-looking man. And the Lord is with him" (1 Samuel 16:15-18).

Notice what sets David apart. Notice what gets him in the king's palace. Yes, he played skillfully. Yes, he was brave, well-spoken, and good-looking. But when you're dealing with evil, those things alone won't work. The attendants realized that "the Lord is with him."

Saul agreed and sent for David to come to the palace and play for him. The Bible says that "whenever the spirit from God came on Saul, David would take up his lyre and play. Then relief would come to Saul; he would feel better, and the evil spirit would leave him" (1 Samuel 16:19-23). This is just the beginning of the effects of the anointing on David's life. The anointing allowed David to play in the King's palace, to defeat Goliath, and to become one of the greatest leaders of one of the greatest nations in history.

- The anointing took David to places he couldn't have gotten to on his own.
- The anointing gave David power over the forces of evil.
- The anointing filled David with boldness and courage.
- The anointing enabled David to conquer enemies.
- The anointing propelled David towards his purpose.

The anointing of Almighty God can do the same for your children. As parents, your children's skill set, gifts, and education will only take them so far. The anointing of the Lord will enable them to achieve all that God has for them.

## Consecration

Let's return to our ecosystem metaphor. An organism cannot be forced to grow. But within the proper ecosystem or atmosphere, both the things that are present (such as water, soil conditions, and food supply) and the things that aren't (such as toxins and bulldozers), create an environment where that organism has the opportunity to grow and thrive. Such is the case with anointing. You can't force a child to receive the anointing. You can, however, help to provide an ecosystem in which your child will be the most receptive to the anointing.

In the Old Testament, when God was getting ready to do something big, he would often say something like, "Consecrate yourselves, for tomorrow the Lord will do amazing things among you."[1] Consecration is the act of setting something apart for the worship or service of God. It is both a separation from sin and a separation to God. When a person would be separated unto the Lord, God's presence and power would rain down upon him or her. Consecration is separation plus saturation. David experienced both. He had a time of separation in the shepherd's field. As he emerged from the field, he was saturated in the anointing. How do our children walk in the anointing and power of God? The same way. Separation plus saturation.

---

David had a time of separation in the shepherd's field. As he emerged from the field, he was saturated in the anointing.

Consecration = Separation + Saturation

---

## SEPARATION

Providing an atmosphere of separation for our children, can get tricky. When I think of my kids hitting puberty and all that entails, the Amish life seems like a viable option. (Or perhaps a monastery. Or both.) While I believe there are individuals whom the Lord calls to lead a life physically separated from others, the path for most people involves learning, as Jesus teaches, to be in the world but not of it.[2]

We don't earn God's anointing (or any other gift for that matter), but we can live our lives in such a way as to be more receptive containers to the gifts and anointing God wants to provide. I want to focus on what, I believe, is one of the biggest determining factors of a life that is receptive to the anointing—purity.

One evening when I was taking a week of classes in Seattle for my doctoral program, my friend Shane and I decided to see a movie. With the options being pretty slim, we opted for a very manly film called "The Huntsman." Ok, full disclosure, it was "Snow White and the Huntsman." But before you tear a corner off of my man card, consider that at least we did leave the customary "open man seat" between us.

It ended up being a cool movie. In one scene, the characters faced a troll-like monster at a bridge. The troll awakens and comes after them with brute force. The huntsman retaliates in kind, telling Snow White to run and then seeks to match the troll blow for blow. It doesn't work. With one swipe, the troll knocks the Huntsman down and approaches for the final blow. At this point, Snow White, who has been hiding behind a rock, comes out and musters a yell loud enough to distract the troll. The troll retaliates with a roar of his own, which knocks the young girl to the ground. She gets up and changes her approach. Knowing that she won't oust the troll with physical strength, she looks directly into his eyes with a look of both kindness and courage. He can't take it. He looks away, and then leaves. In this scene and throughout the movie, we see a glimpse of the power of this young, beautiful girl. Her power is directly tied to her name—Snow White. In other words, her power is in her purity.

The scene reminded me of the story of Samson. If you grew up going to Sunday school, you probably learned that the secret to Samson's strength was his hair. No disrespect here to your Sunday school teacher. I'm sure he or she was a man or woman of God, but they got this one wrong. The secret to Samson's strength wasn't his hair. It was his purity. Samson was a Nazarite, and being a Nazarite meant separation—no grape juice, no killing, and no haircut.

---

The secret to Samson's strength wasn't his hair. It was his purity.

---

Samson's bad haircut was the result of a bad relationship, and that bad relationship was just another wrong decision in a series of wrong decisions. This pathway began when he was a young man, in a relationship with a Philistine woman from Timnah. When his parents objected to Samson marrying her because she was not serving God, he threw a tantrum until he got what he wanted. As it turns out, she tricked him into telling him the answer to a riddle. He threw another tantrum, abandoning her as he went back home to live with his parents. Later, he wanted to return to her, only to find her father had given her in marriage to another.

Years later, we find Samson spending a night with a prostitute in Gaza. Finally, he hooks up with the infamous Delilah, who wears him down and convinces him to reveal the outward secret of his strength. The haircut may have been the final outward act that caused the power drain, but Samson's loss of power began with his loss of sexual purity.

When you lose your separation from sin, you lose your purity. When you lose your purity, you lose your power. The enemy understands this reality. The attack on a generation's sexuality and purity is becoming more and more intense at a younger and younger age. We live in a world where the average age of first exposure to pornography is eleven, and one quarter of sixth through eighth graders have had sexual intercourse.

> When you lose your separation from sin, you lose your purity. When you lose your purity, you lose your power.

This principle isn't just an old covenant thing. Instead of dismissing the importance of sexual purity, Jesus actually raises the standard. "You have heard that it was said, 'You shall not commit adultery.' But I tell you that anyone who looks at a woman lustfully has already committed adultery with her in his heart."[3] Paul tells us in the book of Ephesians, "But among you there must not be even a hint of sexual immorality, or of any kind of impurity, or of greed, because these are improper for God's holy people."[4] Sexual purity matters, both in us as parents and in our children.

While I realize the issue of purity is so much greater than just sexuality, I also recognize that we live in a sex-crazed, sensually-saturated world. Thus, how we teach our children to walk in purity as it relates to sexuality is paramount. Here are a few thoughts on how we can reach this goal, not just with a defensive posture, but by taking initiative to raise children who walk in purity.

1. Your Life and Marriage

This book is about David's childhood, so I don't want to spend much time on his adult years. But in this case, to avoid it would be to miss out on a crucial aspect pertaining to anointing. We saw what happened when Saul lost his anointing. It wasn't pretty. It opened the door for evil and all of the effects thereof. Thankfully because of David's repentant heart, this unraveling didn't happen to David to the same degree it did to Saul. But David did experience a power drain in his life. This decline all hinged around Bathsheba. Before David's lust and adulterous affair, he was in the zone. He enjoyed favor, victory over his enemies, and great expansion of his kingdom. After the affair, he lost a child and experienced great turmoil in his family, which included the rape of one of his daughters and the rebellion of one of his sons.

Parents, your sexual purity matters more than you realize. It affects your children deeply. In fact, David shows us that sexual impurity in our lives breeds vulnerability in our daughters and rebellion in our sons. Purity in our sons and daughters begins with purity in our own lives. David's actions with Bathsheba also show us that nothing will drain a person's anointing and power like sexual impurity.

---

Sexual impurity in our lives breeds vulnerability in our daughters and rebellion in our sons.

---

Perhaps one of the greatest gifts that you can give to your kids in the area of sexuality and purity is to model what a great marriage looks like to your children. You will not be perfect, but with so many horrible examples out there ranging from confusing at best to downright demonic at worst, your kids need to see what a Godly marriage looks like. They need to see you hold hands and hug. They need to see you go on dates. They need to see husbands serving their wives and wives honoring their husbands. Doing this will secure an image in your children's minds that won't quickly be forgotten.

2. First Date

Recently I heard a dad talk about all of the mistakes and mess-ups he had made raising his kids. One of the things he got right was "dating" his daughters when they were young. He would take them out to a nice restaurant. He would open the door for them and treat them like princesses. He would show them how a man is supposed to treat a woman. Now that they are older and of "dating age," he says that when loser boys come shuffling up to them, not knowing how to treat them, his girls turn the other way. Dads, can you say, "Win!" The first "date" that your children should experience is with you.

3. The Internet and Social Media

Hearing just one or two stories about sexting or the ease of access to internet pornography is enough to scare a parent into wanting to run back to the Stone Age. But what do you do? Today's children are a digital native generation, meaning they are the first generation to grow up with technology as a primary language. Your kid knew touching, swiping, and interacting with a screen before he or she could form full sentences. How do you navigate this world?

My good friend and youth pastor at our church, Jon Hernandez, is not only an expert in youth culture, but one of the most brilliant minds I know when it comes to technology. He often teaches parents and gives them some suggestions when it comes to helping their children navigate a digital world. If your children are elementary school age, these probably won't apply yet, but it's coming.

1) Teach how to navigate

While you may be tempted keep your kid from having a driver's license until he or she turns 21, we know that's not a realistic option. So if we can't keep them from the car, then we need to teach them how to drive safely, and to drive to the right destinations. Technology is about the same things: teaching your child how to navigate safely and arrive at good destinations.

2) No screens by yourself

You wouldn't allow someone of the opposite sex into your home and into your child's bedroom with the door closed and locked. Then why would you allow your kid to have a television, computer, or be on a smart phone in his or her room? When it comes to phones, keep the charger in your room. At bedtime, the phone goes into your room to be charged.

3) There's no such thing as privacy

When it comes to technology, your children have no privacy rights. That means, mom and dad, you have the passwords to all of their social media accounts and have the right to check them whenever you want.

4. Teach Your Kids to Have a Picture of Their Future

During a break at a conference, my friend and I decided to run on a trail by a lake. It was a chilly February afternoon, so we got our cold-weather running gear on and set out. I'm what you would call a casual runner, as I run a couple of times a week, basically to stay somewhat in shape and counteract my habit of eating ice cream before bed. My friend Mark is at another level. He was a college track star. Unlike loads of guys who have only stories to show for their glory days, he stays in top shape. When we set out, my goal was to keep up and not collapse. We began to have a conversation, which for Mr. Track Star was not a problem. But all I could do was manage to run and breathe at the same time, much less carry on a conversation. I started to ask him questions for a couple of reasons: First, Mark has four daughters and is a great leader and father, so I wanted to glean wisdom from him. Second, my completing the run without passing out depended on him doing the talking.

Mark shared with me that before his daughters even begin to be allowed to go out with young men, each of them must clearly articulate a list of qualities she wants in a husband. Mark explained that too many young people just wander into dating without a clue. They'll go out with anyone who is cute. But by having his daughters think and pray through what a man of God, someone they can envision spending their lives with, looks like, the chances increase that his daughters won't even give the time of day to someone who doesn't meet those standards.

As I listened, I thought this approach was brilliant. First of all, I have seen, time and time again, amazing young men and women of God settle for second best when dating. Whether out of fear that they'll end up lonely or out of emotional insecurity, they end up surrendering God's best for their lives.

Second, I love how this process teaches our kids to begin to dream God's dream for their lives. As a youth pastor, we would often do some version of a "True Love Waits" campaign. We would teach a series on sexual purity, followed by a ring ceremony whereby, in connection with their parents, the student would make a pledge to remain sexually pure until his or her wedding night. While there were many wonderful things about this type of program, the one thing I always felt was missing was teaching students what to do in the meantime. Teaching our kids to say "no" to the wrong things is good, but perhaps it's even more important to teach them to say "yes" to the right things.

Only one tree was off limits in the Garden of Eden. Adam and Eve were free to eat from all of the other trees. God's "Yes!" is always bigger than God's "No." Just like the serpent of old, the enemy today wants to shift our children's eyes from all they can have to the things they can't. Instead of the teenage years being years of celebrating life and purity, teens often end up trying to get as close to the "no" line as possible without going over the edge. When we teach our kids to dream, to look at the big picture and begin with the end in mind, the "no's" become easier because they understand the why.

---

God's "Yes!" is always bigger than God's "No."

---

## The Source of Purity

While I am convinced that the anointing, both in our lives and in our kids' lives, is tied to our purity, let's not forget the source of that purity. We are not pure in and of ourselves, and we can do nothing to move up the purity scale, even an inch.

Zechariah had a vision of this reality. The account reads:

> Then the angel showed me Jeshua the high priest standing before the angel of the Lord. The Accuser, Satan, was there at the angel's right hand, making accusations against Jeshua. And the Lord said to Satan, "I, the Lord, reject your accusations, Satan. Yes, the Lord, who has chosen Jerusalem, rebukes you. This man is like a burning stick that has been snatched from the fire."
>
> Jeshua's clothing was filthy as he stood there before the angel. So the angel said to the others standing there, "Take off his filthy clothes." And turning to Jeshua he said, "See, I have taken away your sins, and now I am giving you these fine new clothes."[5]

If you've ever spilled coffee down your shirt before an important meeting, or gotten a mustard stain on your dress at a wedding, you can feel just a hint of Jeshua's pain here. Jeshua was standing before Almighty God with filthy clothes. This dilemma wasn't a "slip into the bathroom with a Tide wipe" problem. He was filthy before a holy God, and everyone knew it. To make matters even worse, Satan was right there next to him doing what he does best—accusing us of our failure to measure up to God's standards.

Perhaps the accuser is even in your ear right now. Maybe he's reminding you of some sin or failure from years ago. Or maybe he's making similar accusations in the life of your child—reminding him or her of a past sin. Rest assured, accusations made against sin that is under the blood of Christ aren't accusations against you; they are accusations against Jesus. It's like the enemy telling Jesus, "Jesus, your blood wasn't sufficient. You didn't complete your work on the cross." That's why the accusation is rejected. I love the Lord's reply: "I, the Lord, reject your accusations, Satan."[6] Right now, you can rest assured that any past sins, any past moral failures, any past times of rebellion, are all completely covered by the blood of Christ, and the Lord himself has rejected all accusations against you.

> Accusations made against sin that is under the blood of Christ aren't accusations againt you; they are accusations against Jesus.

The response doesn't just stop with the dismissal of the accusation. Jeshua gets a brand-new wardrobe! His sins weren't just covered up; they were completely removed. And he was given a brand-new set of clothes!

We are only made pure through the blood of Jesus Christ. We are clothed in his righteousness. And we can only remain pure through that blood and the power of the Holy Spirit.

## SATURATION

Let's go back to our definition of consecration. It is separation (both from sin and to God) plus saturation. While purity is one of the key conditions that allows a child to be receptive to the anointing, it is not enough. The individual needs to be immersed in the power of the Holy Spirit. Remember that first, David was separated in the field. Then he was saturated in the anointing.

I'm not sure what your church tradition is when you "anoint" people, but in my tribe, we generally put a small portion of oil on a person's forehead. That's not what David experienced. Samuel would have taken a horn of oil and poured it over David's head. David would have been walking back to the shepherd's field drenched, with oil running down his hair, face, and clothes. He would have been saturated.

In the Old Testament, the Holy Spirit came upon certain people at certain times for certain purposes. Bezalel and Oholiab were filled with the Spirit for artistic expression and giftings in the building of the Temple. Joseph was filled with the Spirit for dream interpretations and wisdom to govern. Moses and the elders were filled with the Spirit to prophesy and equip them for leadership. Joshua was filled with the Spirit to succeed Moses and lead Israel into the Promised Land. We could also tell the stories of Daniel, Elijah, Elisha, Isaiah, and many others.

After the death and resurrection of Jesus, the Holy Spirit was made available to everyone all of the time. On the day of Pentecost, when those in the Upper Room were baptized in the Holy Spirit, Peter stood and addressed the crowd, referring to the prophecy from Joel. He said:

> Fellow Jews and all of you who live in Jerusalem, let me explain this to you; listen carefully to what I say. These people are not drunk, as you suppose. It's only nine in the morning! No, this is what was spoken by the prophet Joel:
>
> In the last days, God says,
>   I will pour out my Spirit on all people.
> Your sons and daughters will prophesy,
>   your young men will see visions,
>   your old men will dream dreams.

Even on my servants, both men and women,
I will pour out my Spirit in those days,
and they will prophesy.

I will show wonders in the heavens above
and signs on the earth below...[7]

Just a few weeks prior, this same Peter was following Jesus from a distance, cowering in fear and cursing to a teenage girl, denying that he was a disciple of Christ. Now, having been immersed in the power of the Holy Spirit, Peter stands boldly before the masses, preaching the gospel of Christ, and seeing 3000 people saved in one day. For our children to live in the fullness of the anointing and power of God, they too, must be saturated in the Holy Spirit.

## My Story

In all my years of serving Christ, understanding what it means to live a Spirit-empowered life has more greatly transformed me than any other single event. While I was raised in a wonderful Christian home by amazing Christian parents, the problem came in my sophomore year in high school. I didn't ever stop loving Jesus; I just didn't hate sin. I thought I could do both. I figured I could serve Jesus on Sundays and at home, but at school and on weekends, I found myself wanting to fit in so badly that I ended up with the wrong crowd and wrong lifestyle. To be honest, this lifestyle was fun at first. Sin is fun, for a season. But the downward spiral quickly escalated, and I became miserable. I wanted to turn from sin, but I seemed powerless to do so.

The summer of my junior year, I ended up on a mission trip to the Dominican Republic. In a service in a small church outside of Santo Domingo, one of the youth pastors leading our trip, Pastor Jim

Grove, was preaching on being filled with the Holy Spirit. He gave an altar call for people who wanted to receive the baptism of the Holy Spirit. I was just kind of hanging out in the back when Pastor Jim approached me and asked if I had been filled with the Holy Spirit. I said that I hadn't. He and several other people laid their hands on me. I will never forget falling to my knees under the power of God on that sweltering August morning, being immersed in the Holy Spirit and receiving my prayer language, or what is sometimes referred to as speaking in tongues. I'm not saying I was perfect afterwards, but this moment forever changed the trajectory of my life. I was filled with a new power to love and serve God at a higher capacity than I ever thought possible.

Parents, I realize that many different theological viewpoints exist regarding what it means to be empowered by the Holy Spirit. The purpose of this book is not to elevate one stance or condemn another. But from what I experienced in my own life, I can tell you that this infilling has taken my relationship with Christ to a greater level. My encouragement to you would be to search the scriptures, your own heart, and the wisdom of others on what living a Spirit-empowered life means both for yourself and your children.

## Vigorous Young Olive Trees

One of the verses I routinely pray over my children is Psalm 128:3: "Your children will be like vigorous young olive trees as they sit around your table." First of all, notice the connection again to the table. Apparently David (now the father and not the son) realized the importance of having children around the table. Even before I knew what this verse meant (I'm not sure I've ever seen an olive tree), it sounded like a cool thing to pray over my kids. This verse seemed to carry a sense of raising strong kids, so it seemed like a good thing to pray. Then, when I started to study what olive branches represent, I found olive branches are symbols of:

victory
abundance
glory
peace
wisdom
fertility
power
anointing

Wow! These traits seemed like an amazing list to pray for my kids. (Well, not the fertility part. At least not now. Later. But not now.) As I pray this verse over my children, it has an even richer and fuller meaning.

I recently completed a unique fast. While it's not something specifically mentioned in scripture, I felt prompted by the Lord to do a three-day fast simply around the elements of communion and anointing—bread, grape juice, and olive oil. These elements symbolize the broken body of our Savior and the anointing of the Holy Spirit. As I took time to receive communion at each meal (along with the dipping of the bread in the olive oil), I was both reminded of the power of the cross of Christ and the power of the anointing of the Holy Spirit. One of my prayers during this time had to do with "vigorous young olive trees":

*I pray that my children live in the fullness of the victory of Christ.*

*I pray that my children live in overflow and abundance, that they may have more than enough to be a blessing to their city.*

*I pray that my children know and live in God's glory.*

*I pray that my children live in peace with God, others, and themselves.*

*I pray that my children walk in wisdom.*

*I pray for my children's future spouses and children. I pray that they would enter into the marriage covenant sexually pure and that they would remain pure to each other. I pray their families and children would be blessed.*

*I pray that my children know and walk in God's power.*

*I pray that my children are saturated in the anointing of the Holy Spirit.*

Imagine young David returning to the field after having just been anointed by the prophet Samuel. He couldn't possibly have known all this would mean. He probably had no clue he would defeat Goliath, become the greatest king of one of the greatest nations on earth, and become a prominent part of the lineage of the Messiah. But I bet he felt something. "From that day on the Spirit of the Lord came powerfully upon David." Like Peter Parker getting bit by a spider, I imagine he noticed a difference.

Parents, again, what will be *the* defining mark upon our children? Wouldn't it be great for it to be the anointing of the Lord? In fact, why not stop and pray right now that your children will be saturated in the anointing of Almighty God. Pray that your children would be "olive branches around your table."

# GROUP DISCUSSION GUIDE

1) Consecration = Separation + Saturation. What are the four initiatives offered by the author to inspire a life of separation (purity) for your child(ren)? How close are you to accomplishing those initiatives? What additional lifestyle changes need to be implemented toward these goals? Share with the group any additional initiatives that have worked well for you.
2) What are some of the challenges you have faced when it comes to sexual purity for your child(ren)? What steps have you made to keep the atmosphere in your home sexually pure?
3) If your child is of dating age, how are you guiding him or her into having the highest of standards both for whom they choose to date and their commitment to sexual purity?
4) Review the three suggestions for cultivating purity in an online world. How have you implemented safeguards for your child(ren)?
5) What are ways you can be a vessel God uses to help saturate your child(ren) with God's anointing? Develop a prayer of consecration to use as you pray and speak words of life into their spirit(s). Search for scriptures to pray over your child(ren) daily. Ask the Holy Spirit to lead, guide, and direct you as you consecrate yourself to do these things for your children.

# 5

## A Child Who has a Playful Spirit

*So he sent for him and had him brought in.*
*He was ruddy and had [bright] eyes.*

*(1 Samuel 16:12)*

Whatever happened to recess? You know, the highlight of every kid's day. The reason for a third grader's existence. The portal through the double doors at the end of the hallway, leading to a magical world of sunshine, pump-swings, monkey-bars, and kickball. After a grueling morning of multiplication tables and spelling tests, recess offered an escape into a land that enlivens the heart and replenishes the soul.

I can still remember kickball on the blacktop when I was in Mrs. Grazetti's second-grade class, or football games at Victory Elementary School while in Mr. McVay's fifth-grade class. I remember Billy

Wright running fantastic routes. I remember pretending I was John Elway and hoping the other team would rush the QB so I'd have a chance to run.

Maybe there was a teacher or two watching over us, but it was largely unstructured play. And we survived under our own supervision, didn't we? Sure, picking teams took way too long, and yes, we experienced NFL replay-like delays in the middle of the games while we argued over whether someone had called "no bunting" or not. But we figured it out. We didn't need three referees, a new scoreboard, five specialty coaches for each team, a team mom, and twenty-eight parents hanging over the fence all coaching their kids from the sidelines.

Today, we've largely removed recess from our children. No, I'm not talking about the twenty minutes of outdoor play at school; I'm talking about the concept of *unstructured* play. What used to be building ramps and jumping bikes in the backyard has become five-year-olds racing motocross. What used to be shooting hoops with the neighborhood kids on a rickety, old bucket until your mom called you in for dinner is now an all-day Saturday basketball league. What used to be splashing and swimming in the creek on a hot summer day is now a swimming program at the Y. What used to be little girls playing dress-up with their dolls is now moms playing dress-up using their little girls as dolls.

The way we've altered the wisdom of the ages when it comes to childhood is shocking. We are seemingly pushing our kids to *grow up, grow up, grow up*. We want them to know their ABC's, colors, and numbers before they enter preschool. We want them to read before Kindergarten. We want them to know a language, take piano, master dance, and be on the traveling soccer team before first grade. From the time a kid hits three, we're panicked that if they aren't reading soon, they'll fall behind the rest of the kids. Then they'll probably get picked on, not get into college, and live a life of crime on the streets. So take away the toy truck, and let's start working on those phonics!

We are in need of multiple revivals in America—one of them is a revival of "recess"—unstructured play. In recess, children learn to work together and problem solve. Recess gives kids the opportunity to make the lineup and decide what to do when the football hits the telephone wire. In recess, they learn to argue, get mad, and then be best friends again by the time they line up at the water fountain. In recess, they learn that not everyone gets picked first, and not every kid gets a ribbon.

---

We are in need of multiple revivals in America—one of them is a revival of "recess"—unstructured play.

---

## Rosy Cheeks and Sparkling Eyes

What does "play" have to do with David's boyhood? Great question. Let's go back to our story. After Samuel had passed over Jesse's sons, David was brought in from the field. Samuel then describes his appearance: "He was glowing with health and had a fine appearance and handsome features." (1 Samuel 16:12, NIV). The ESV reads, "Now he was ruddy and had beautiful eyes and was handsome."

The words used to describe David's physical appearance are actually just as informative about David's inner person as they are about his Esquire good looks. Not to dismiss the fact that David was apparently a handsome guy, but the description goes deeper.

First, David is described as "ruddy." The Hebrew word used here is *adomi*. The root of the word is from "adom" which means reddish of the hair or the complexion. It means "to show blood in the face, i.e. flush or turn rosy[1] and carries the connotation of youth.[2] In other words, think of a young boy who has just come in from playing outside. His cheeks are flushed with youthful energy and a playful spirit.

David is also described as having "beautiful eyes." I'd like to suggest there's more to this than having perfect Alec-Baldwin-blue eyes. It wasn't just about David's looks; it was about his outlook. There's something about the eyes. Think of someone who has a sparkle in their eyes. Think of someone who always seems to be smiling with their eyes. Eyes have the ability to reveal life, energy, and vitality. They are indeed a window to the soul.

We might expect David, having just come in from working in the field and having just been overlooked, to appear tired, worn-out, discouraged, and downtrodden. But that's not how he's described. In fact, the portrayal is quite the opposite. David is described as "glowing with health," "ruddy," and having "beautiful eyes." Translation: as David came in from the field, he displayed a youthful energy, a playful spirit, and a boyish zeal for life.

As David came in from the field, he displayed a youthful energy, a playful spirit, and a boyish zeal for life.

I realize I'm using creative license here, but I don't think it's a stretch. I don't think David was in the field sulking and pouting that he had to work. I think he found time to play—building forts and playing "attack of the Philistines." I think in the midst of tending sheep, he found ways to use his imagination. Somehow I suspect that when he led the sheep to a watering hole, he tore off his robe and did a cannonball into the cool water.

That's what our kids need more of. We need more kids coming in from the outdoors with their cheeks flushed and eyes sparkling. We need more kids giggling on swing sets and climbing trees. We need more play.

## A Playful Spirit

We were at a graduation party for the son of close family friends on a bright, sunny, May Carolina afternoon. Now, we Carolinians know how to do a picnic, and we definitely know how to do BBQ—pulled pork, Eastern NC style with vinegar-based sauce and red slaw, washed down with Sun Drop or sweet tea. After eating, the younger kids started playing wiffle ball, and I joined in. My friend Dan did too. Now I'm not 25 anymore, so I was proud of myself for staying somewhat youthful. But Dan took it to a whole new level. At 65, he was running, throwing, even diving! (Actually it was more of a "stumble-and-roll," but hey, we'll call it a dive!) Dan is a successful accountant and businessman. He is involved in a lot of "serious" stuff. I'm convinced that one of the reasons he is successful is because he was out there playing wiffle ball. Even at a more "advanced" age, Dan has eyes that sparkle and a playful spirit.

My dad exhibits these qualities as well. One winter night I called him around 9:00 pm, and he didn't answer. When he called back, he apologized for not getting my call. He was outside sledding. Oh yeah, did I mention he was 70? My dad grew up playing outside, and he's never let that fade. He tried surfing for the first time at 74. He plays volleyball weekly with people half his age. He is continually outdoors biking, walking, or swimming. He's never let anything deter his playful energy.

I love being around people who know how to have fun. I bet you do too. There are people who are just great to be around because they make you feel better and make the day better. I want that kind of mindset for my kids. I want them to always maintain their inner-kindergartener and never lose their playful zeal for life. How do you raise kids who are "ruddy" and have "bright eyes"? Let's take a look.

## "Go Outside and Play"

When I finished my doctoral degree, we went to graduation near Portland, Oregon. After the ceremony, we spent several days in a cabin at the base of Mt. Hood, a 45-minute drive from the Columbia River Gorge. This stretch of land may be one of the most beautiful places on Earth—80 miles of emerald-green forests and waterfalls, all along a 4000-foot canyon.

Every day we would hike and look at waterfalls. Along one such hike, I came across a sign. It read: "Who Needs an Avatar? In today's high-tech world, many of our children are disconnected from nature. Recent scientific findings support the parental refrain—'Go outside and play!'"

I decided to follow up on those "recent scientific findings." Turns out, the sign was right! We hear a lot about kids diagnosed with ADD (or ADHD), but Richard Louv, Chairman of the Children & Nature Network Board of Directors, says kids are actually suffering from NDD (Nature Deficit Disorder). According to one study, 71 percent of today's mothers reported playing outdoors every day as children, while only 26 percent have kids who play outdoors daily. This isn't just city kids. The results are surprisingly similar for rural families.[3] These findings are shocking if you think about it. Only 1 in 4 kids you meet today will have biked, climbed a tree, thrown a ball, or played on a swing set within any given 24-hour period.

The study explains that the culprit of Nature Deficit Disorder is a "growing demand on children's time, resulting in less free and unstructured outdoor playtime." [The study] says that our kids' playtime has become "increasingly structured."[4]

The problem is not just lack of outdoor play. The problem is lack of free play. Today, even when kids are outdoors, adults are standing over their shoulders, hovering, covering, and smothering with blankets of supervision and organization. You've heard, "There's an app for that." We could probably now say, "There's a league for that." Kids don't just need to be outside. They need to be outside in an *unstructured* environment. They need to be riding their bikes and building forts. They need to be exploring in the woods. They need to be playing kickball and stickball in backyards and cul-de-sacs.

"Go outside and play" has been replaced by:

"Go get your soccer uniform," or
"Go get your ballet shoes," or
"Go put on your football cleats."

Unfortunately, play has become a league to sign up for rather than a natural part of childhood.

Unfortunately, play has become a league to sign up for rather than a natural part of childhood.

*But it's kind of the same thing, right? They're still getting exercise outdoors.* That assumption is the danger. No, it's not the same at all. In fact, Dr. Peter Gray in his article, "The Decline of Play and Rise in Children's Mental Disorders," connects lack of unstructured play to the rise in anxiety and depression. He writes:

> Free play and exploration are, historically, the means by which children learn to solve their own problems, control their own lives, develop their own interests, and become competent in

> pursuit of their own interests. In fact, play, by definition, is activity controlled and directed by the players; and play, by definition, is directed toward intrinsic rather than extrinsic goals.
>
> By depriving children of opportunities to play on their own, away from direct adult supervision and control, we are depriving them of opportunities to learn how to take control of their own lives. We may think we are protecting them, but in fact we are diminishing their joy, diminishing their sense of self-control, preventing them from discovering and exploring the endeavors they would most love, and increasing the odds that they will suffer from anxiety, depression, and other disorders.[5]

Parents, the phrase "Go outside and play" may be one of the most important things you can tell your children. Play isn't just a break from life; play is an essential part of life. Recess is not an escape from learning. Recess is learning. Researchers are confirming that "play in nature, particularly during the critical period of middle childhood, appears to be an especially important time for developing the capacities for creativity, problem-solving, and emotional and intellectual development."[6] As Stuart Brown, author of *Play: How it Shapes the Brain, Opens the Imagination, and Invigorates the Soul,* says, "Play leads to brain plasticity, adaptability, and creativity." He goes on to say, "Nothing fires up the brain like play."[7]

---

The phrase "Go outside and play" may be one of the most important things you can tell your children.

---

The study goes on to list some of the further benefits of outdoor play:

- Nature-smart kids get higher test scores
- Classroom behavior is better if children have recess
- Children with ADHD functioned better in the woods than indoors
- Children benefit from appropriate risk-taking during outdoor play
- Nearby nature reduces stress in children
- Nearby nature boosts children's cognitive functioning
- Access to nature nurtures self-discipline[8]

In other words,

> Want your kids to be smart?
> "Go outside and play."
> Want your kids to be healthy?
> "Go outside and play."
> Want your kids to be creative?
> "Go outside and play."
> Want your kids to be good problem-solvers?
> "Go outside and play."
> Want your kids to be successful in relationships and in life?
> "Go outside and play."

I hope this truth is extremely stress-relieving for you to hear. Desiring to see our children succeed, we parents often feel pressured to get kids involved in organized activities at a young age. We feel pressured to fill our calendars and structure the week with karate, ballet, and soccer. Summers have become weeks of baseball camps and swimming lessons. Please hear this: according to research, the best way for your child to develop the skill sets needed to succeed is not through organized activities, but through having the freedom to be a kid!

God hardwired kids to play. It's in play that they learn life skills and have fun doing it. Wow, doesn't that feel great?! One of your biggest jobs as a parent is to tell your kids, "Go outside and play!"

## TRIPLE RECESS, HIGHER TEST SCORES

One elementary school in Fort Worth, Texas is discovering the power of play firsthand. This year, Eagle Mountain Elementary began tripling the time for recess, from 20 minutes to an hour. And they started focusing on character development in addition to building skill sets. The program, scheduled to be implemented in other schools in Texas, California, and Oklahoma, was launched by Texas Christian University kinesisiologist, Debbie Rhea. Rhea had the idea after seeing the Finnish school system first-hand, which continually ranks at or near the top in international education rankings. At first, two first grade teachers with a combined six decades of teaching experience were nervous about fitting everything in the school day. But now, they're raving fans, saying that halfway through the school year, the kids were way ahead of schedule. According to an article on NPR, Teachers at Eagle Mountain say they've seen a huge transformation in their students. They say kids are less distracted, they make more eye contact, and they tattle less."[9]

Ohio State researcher Bob Murray has the data to back up Eagle Mountain's experience. He says that brain imaging confirms that kids learn better following physical activity and *unstructured* play. He and his colleagues suggest, "Kids with regular recess behave better, are physically healthier and exhibit stronger social and emotional development."[10]

---

Kids with regular recess behave better, are physically healthier and exhibit stronger social and emotional development.

---

Rhea implores, "We keep thinking as adults that we need to control the way [kids] do things. I wish we'd get out of that. They know how to play, they know how to structure their own play — they need that time to grow responsibly." When it comes down to it, Rhea says, "our kids are better off if we just let them be kids."

## Less Noise and More Green

J.R.R. Tolkien is arguably one of the best loved and most widely read authors of the last century, possibly the last millennium. His *Lord of the Rings* trilogy was voted the "book of the millennium" in numerous polls. As you watch Peter Jackson's adaptation of the series to film, one of the striking aspects is the beauty of the scenery. Filmed in Jackson's homeland of New Zealand, The Shire, for instance, is nestled among rolling green hills. Flowers, streams, and sunshine give it Eden-like qualities.

Where did Tolkien get the inspiration for The Shire? It came from his boyhood days in Sarehole, a small hamlet in the British countryside. Tolkien spent part of his childhood roaming and exploring that countryside. As Tolkien penned the beginning of The Hobbit, he recalled Sarehole and had it begin on a morning "long ago in the quiet of the world when there was less noise and more green."[11]

Later in Tolkien's life, he would speak of his boyhood in the countryside of Sarehole, calling it "the longest-seeming and most formative part of my life." What fueled the imagination and creativity behind what would become the millennium's most beloved and best-selling book? It wasn't a children's writing league. It wasn't a private writing tutor. It was a childhood spent playing outside.

Still skeptical of the power of the outdoors? Take ten seconds, close your eyes, and go to your happy place. Ok, now what picture was there? Was there any linoleum? Were there walls without windows? Was there a lot of plastic? How about your phone? Was it there? I'm guessing probably none of the above. And unless you just watched *Happy Gilmore* on TBS, I'm guessing there probably weren't juggling clowns on unicycles either. My hunch is that the scene was filled with palm trees, white beaches, and sunshine. Or perhaps there were mountains with towering evergreens. Or maybe the picture was a sparkling pool, a glass of iced tea, and a great book. I'm guessing that for the majority, your "happy place" was outside. We know it instinctively, don't we? We know we're happier outdoors. That's true for your child as well.

## The Great Outdoors

I had the privilege of growing up in a field. Well, not literally. We did have a house. But the house was in a field. And that field was between two farmer's fields, and those two fields were between miles and miles of woods. Yes, a few other houses were around, but not many. We were about four miles from the nearest stoplight and thirty miles from the nearest sizable grocery store. And I loved our field.

That field was the sight of some momentous sporting events. We experienced championship football games, down-to-the-wire basketball games, walk-off home runs, and diving plays in the hole at shortstop. Those moments were pretty amazing considering the only players were my mom, my dad, my brother, and me.

Fall Sunday afternoons during football season were spent playing two-on-two football. Summer days were spent with my brother and me shooting hoops on the basketball goal. Summer nights were spent with mom and dad, who took turns pitching to my brother and me. (Yes, mom too. She had an amazing arm, making for a good righty and lefty duo with my dad!)

Even our Little League field was in a field. From our house (remember the rural description), you had to go *another* four miles, turn down a dirt road, and go yet another mile. Off that dirt road in a field was a place where baseball dreams came true.

There were no lights. No multi-sports complexes. Just a field where kids could play and be kids. Those carefree childhood memories still bring a smile to my face. They were years of great joy that have fueled my life into adulthood. During difficult seasons in my life, I have drawn strength from them.

Twice a year, my brother and I load up the vehicles with our spouses and six cousins to go visit Grandpa back in that Pennsylvania field. It's a child's playground extraordinaire. There is a barn with a hayloft. There's a tractor and a four wheeler with miles and miles of paths through fields and woods. One path in particular leads through cornfields and opens onto beautiful towering pines that provide a canopy over trails for walking, rocks for climbing, and a hillside that leads to a gurgling creek. There's even a hunting cabin with a tire swing and zip line.

When we return to North Carolina, things are a bit more limited. Someday we'd like to own more land, but for now, we're on 0.23 acres in a neighborhood, forcing us to be more creative. Fortunately, our home does back up to woods, and I've cleared some of it for additional play space. And we live at the end of a cul-de-sac, so our circle has become a baseball diamond, kickball field, bike riding trail, and more.

Perhaps you find yourself in the same situation of living in a city or a neighborhood that is not as conducive to outdoor play. But you can find ways to be creative and get your kids outdoors. For instance, you can take advantage of parks and green spaces. More and more towns and cities are doing a better and better job of providing nature trails, greenways, and parks for recreation. Or you can schedule some unstructured outdoor playtime at grandma's house, or on a friend's property. Or load up and go camping. Just remember this principle: You don't have to own it to enjoy it.

## The Cure for Myopia

In recent years, myopia, or nearsightedness, has become increasingly common in children. While the cause(s) of myopia are still up for debate, a child's environment seems to be an important factor. Recent studies point to "lack of outdoor play" as a potential factor for myopia.

These findings are fascinating on a number of levels physiologically, but perhaps even more so metaphorically. Nearsightedness means that you are able to see things clearly up close, but things far away become blurry. What is one of the "knocks" on this generation? Selfish? Entitled? They only see things that are "up close"? Perhaps we have raised not only a physically myopic generation but a spiritually myopic generation as well.

Want your kids to see far and dream big? Want your kids to not only be concerned with their world but also with the worlds of others? Want your kids to look at the horizon of life and imagine what possibilities are out there to be explored and discovered? Then, "Go outside and play."

## A Lesson from a Boy and a Tiger

I love reading Calvin and Hobbes. Calvin embodies the spirit of childhood and play. He's forever pretending to zoom off to other planets in spaceships, playing tag, pestering the neighbor girl, Susie, up in a tree house, or running around pretending to defeat bad guys. Recently, my brother texted me a picture of Calvin and Hobbes that had a major impact on me. The drawing was of Calvin as a gown up. He was in a suit and tie, carrying a briefcase, and his head was hung with a sad expression was on his face. In the thought bubble over his head was a childhood memory of he and Hobbes in a wagon, zooming downhill, joyful expressions of bliss and freedom radiating from their faces. I don't ever want to get to the place in my life where I forget to play. And I don't ever want to fill my children's lives with so many activities that they don't have those kinds of exuberant memories from their own childhood.

## Permission to Play

I was in Florida for some important meetings at a university. I was driving from the school to the hotel and was a bit stressed. I don't remember exactly what the problem was, but I'm sure it had to do with some budget or people issues at work. As I turned from Longfellow Boulevard onto North Crystal Lake, I started checking voice messages. One was from my daughter Ana who was four at the time.

"Daddy," she said in her sweet, little-girl voice. "I hope you have a good time. And I hope you go swimming. And I hope you eat ice cream. And I hope you take a shower." A smile came across my face. That was exactly what I needed to hear. I needed permission to play. As silly as it might sound, receiving permission to play from a four-year-old released me from stress and allowed me to enjoy my week. So I went swimming. And I ate ice cream. And yes, I took a shower too!

You may not think this is the case, but your kids need permission to play. They need your blessing. And mom and dad, they need to see you play too. Yes, I know life is serious. I know there are real problems, real challenges, and real difficulties. But it's amazing what can happen when we maintain a playful spirit. I bet you need permission to play more. And I bet your kids do too.

So, I hope you always go swimming.
And I hope you always eat ice cream.
(And yes, I hope you always take a shower!)

## GROUP DISCUSSION GUIDE

1) Think back to your childhood. What are some of your best memories as a kid of playing outside?
2) How much time does your child spend each day in outdoor, unstructured play?
3) What are some local cost-free properties/outdoor activities where you could offer "go outside and play" opportunities for your child(ren)?
4) What are some "intentional" activities you can make happen to create nostalgic outdoor memories for your family that will have impact and influence on your family for years to come? Purpose to place time on your calendar for outdoor, unstructured play with your kids.
5) Identify some possible "myopic" characteristics you have developed or that your child(ren) may be developing? How can you bring "corrective vision" to those situations?
6) Adopt the "Permission to Play" for your family or better yet, create one of your own!

# 6

## A Child Who Chooses Faith-Adventure

*David asked the men standing near him, "...Who is this uncircumcised Philistine that he should defy the armies of the living God?"*

*(1 Samuel 17:26)*

Recently I watched a video about Jedidiah Jenkins, a teacher from California who decided to quit his job and spend a year riding (and living from) his bicycle from Oregon to Patagonia, the region comprising the southern end of South America.[1] The video itself is captivating as you watch clips of Jedidiah riding through snow-capped mountains, swinging off a rope swing into a lake, and exploring a thrilling new view with every twist and turn in the road. It's a great story and a really well-done short film. Describing his adventure, he narrates:

> When you're a kid, everything is astonishing. Everything is new. Your brain is awake. Every passing second, your brain is learning something new, learning how the world works, and so the muscle of your brain is activated. As you get older and your brain has figured out the patterns of the way the world works … and establishes routine, the alertness goes away. … I think that's what travel in general does. It wakes up your brain. I'll go into a new country … and I'll find it beautiful and shocking. … I want to be aware of every day that I'm alive. I want to make it to 85 and be exhausted because I have been alive and awake every single day.
>
> When you're a kid, everything's new so you don't have to work for it. You're just astonished by it. Once you're an adult, that's a choice. You choose adventure for your own life. But it's not about the bike. It's about getting out of your routine. … And that's why I'm doing this bike trip, because I don't want my days to control me. … I want to control my days. I want to choose the adventures that I go on. And I want to choose a mind and a soul that's wide awake, because that's what turns your hundred years on this planet into a thousand.

I love the phrases that Jedidiah uses to explain the "why" behind his adventure. He speaks of living wide-awake, living with awe and wonder, and living an adventure. And I love that he recognizes this outlook to be the natural state of children.

Most of parenting involves us teaching our children. But in matters of faith and adventure, the roles are reversed—our children teach us. In this area, the best advice I can give to parents is to get out of the way and let them lead.

This chapter is about doing just that—getting out of the way. It's about learning from your child and letting him or her lead you into a journey of curiosity, discovery, and faith-adventure. These things are already within your child. Our responsibility is to continue to cultivate the ecosystem where these characteristics can grow and thrive.

## DAVID AND FAITH-ADVENTURE

When Goliath appeared for his daily taunting of the Israelites, two different questions were asked. Everyone around David was asking the wrong question: "Have you seen the giant?" Their question revealed their focus. Their eyes were locked on the obstacle. David's brothers and the rest of Saul's army were focused on the problem, and so life became blurry. Their eyesight was bad. When our eyesight is bad, we look down in shame, look back in regret, or look away in fear.

David asked a different question—the right question. To the nearby soldiers, David asked, "Who is this pagan Philistine anyway, that he is allowed to defy the armies of the living God?" Translation: While everyone else was asking, "Have you seen the size of the giant?" David was asking, "Have you seen the size of my God?"

While everyone else was asking, "Have you seen the size of the giant?" David was asking, "Have you seen the size of my God?"

David's question was one of possibility. While his brother's eyes were locked on the problem, David saw potential. He saw past the giant to faith in God and what the Lord could do on his behalf. How did David develop this quality? My theory is that he didn't so much "develop" it as he didn't unlearn it. Have you ever seen a child struggle with belief? Have you ever known a child to have a shortage of faith? In David's shepherd-field years, he wasn't around negative people who felt it was their duty to bring him back to reality and tell him what God couldn't do. He emerged from the field believing that his God could do anything.

Perhaps, like David, we need a healthy theology of faith and adventure. When God created this amazing, wild, and wonderful world, his charge to Adam and Eve was to "be fruitful and multiply. Fill the earth and govern it."[2] In other words, part of this command was, "Go exploring. Go discover. Go live an adventure." Author Mark Batterson says that every "*ology*" is a branch of theology. A belief in God is at the core of discovering the world around us.

God wired us for discovery and adventure. When we are continually learning, discovering, and growing, we are living the life that He intended for us to live. I've seen teenagers grow bored in their relationship with God. Perhaps that's because too many people are questioning their faith instead of discovering it. The word *disciple* literally means "learner". If our kids are truly to be disciples of Christ, then part of our job is to be curators of their curiosity.

---

Perhaps too many people are questioning their faith instead of discovering it.

---

The title of this chapter uses the term "faith-adventure," because the two go hand-in-hand. It's what I call the "faith-adventure spiral". Because David believed in his God, he had the amazing experience of defeating Goliath. And because he defeated a nine-foot champion, you better believe his faith increased. When you have great faith, you have greater adventures. And when you have great adventures, you have greater faith. Here's a few suggestions on how to cultivate a great faith-adventure ecosystem:

1) Encourage Your Kids to Keep Asking Questions

If you want the right answers, you have to ask the right questions. Consider this: economic students no longer read the insights of Adam Smith. Psych professors don't have their students study the answers Freud proposed. But political philosophy students still read Plato, Aristotle, and Locke. Why? The reason isn't because the political philosophy guys came up with great answers; rather it's because they asked great questions. Socrates taught by using *elenchus,* which was the combination of story and questions. In almost 40% of his sermons, Jesus was asking questions. Asking questions is important. Asking the right questions is really important.

One of the great things about children is they don't have to be taught how to ask questions. It's intuitive.

*Are we there yet?*
*Where did all the dinosaurs go?*
*Where is my doll?*
*Why is the sky blue?*
*Can I go over to my friend's house?*
*Where do babies come from?*
*Are we there yet?*
*Why is the ocean salty?*
*Are we there yet?*
*Why?*
*Are we there yet?*
*Why?*
*Why?*
*Why?*

If you walk into a Kindergarten classroom, you walk into a world that is wide awake with curiosity and wonder. You will see kids with their hands wrapped around crayons, fingers dipped in paint, and arms raised in the air asking all sorts of questions. For kindergarteners, each day is a blank canvas upon which they can discover something new and create something fantastic.

If you were to leave that room and walk into an eighth grade algebra classroom, most likely you would see a different scenario. You would probably see eyes that are glazed-over from boredom, some heads jerking as they struggle to stay awake, and gazes looking at the clock to see how much longer they must endure the class period. I'm not mad at math teachers. I'm sure there are some terrific ones who make learning interesting and fun. But you understand my point.

While there are multiple reasons for the above descriptions, perhaps one of the main differences is that one is a classroom of "asking" while the other one is a classroom of "telling." In her wonderful book, *Brain-Based Worship*, my doctoral colleague Paula Champion-Jones sheds some light on the development of these differences. She writes, "In 1963, a new philosophy of learning, *reception learning*, ... spread the idea that the brain is nothing more than a container into which information is poured. According to this theory, people do not 'discover' knowledge; knowledge is given to them."[3] Ouch. Perhaps the core of our educational model has been flawed for decades. Perhaps we need to re-discover discovery.

The classroom of telling uses a lecture model. The teacher and the textbook have already done the fun part of discovery. Now they are downloading all of the information into the kids' heads, hoping they'll remember it long enough to pass the test. The classroom of asking begins with questions and possibilities. The kids are given a problem to figure out and a mystery to solve. They get to interact and be a part of the process. In doing the latter, they move from merely memorizing to really learning.

One of the best things we can do as parents is to cultivate our child's inner kindergartener. If we can cultivate their love for discovery, we will do them a world of good and keep them open to a world of possibilities.

One of the best things we can do as parents is to cultivate our child's inner kindergartener. If we can cultivate their love for discovery, we will do them a world of good and keep them open to a world of possibilities.

In the hidden shepherd's field, David didn't have a professor or podcasts. But he did have his curiosity. You can imagine David lying under the stars at night thinking about the vastness and creativity of God. Perhaps those nights tending sheep were inspiration for poems such as:

*The heavens declare the glory of God;*
*the skies proclaim the work of his hands.*[4]

However David's childhood played out in the field, we can safely assume those years were years of discovery and adventure, in part because David emerged asking questions. He began asking, "What if..." "What if someone actually stood up to the bullying taunts of the giant? What if the giant was defeated? What if Israel was free again to enjoy the land God had given them?"

"What if?" It's a question that can change the world. It's a question that can spur dreams and ignite imagination. And it's a question that can be cultivated by incorporating a couple of important dynamics into your child's life.

> "What if?" It's a question that can change the world. It's a question that can spur dreams and ignite imagination.

When it comes to questions of faith, instead of feeling you have to have all the answers, why not encourage discovery? Instead of being a parent who tells your child everything, why not be a parent who helps your child ask great questions? Guide them in the process of discovery for themselves. Show them how to look in the Bible for answers. Teach them to ask God questions and listen for the voice of the Holy Spirit. (And when all else fails, there's still Google!)

2) Make Reading Fun-damental

A morning of Saturday detention during my eleventh grade year was one of the best things that could have happened to me. I won't get into the reasons for the punishment as I've told enough self-effacing stories already. And no, I'm certainly not advocating that you want your kid in detention. But hear me out. For starters, we were few in numbers; we had to spread out (one per table); and we weren't allowed to talk. So, no, my day didn't turn out to be anything like *The Breakfast Club*.[5]

As I sat in the cafeteria at a round table by myself for four hours on a Saturday morning, I was bored out of my mind. For some reason, I either didn't have much homework or had already finished, so I sat there staring at a thick novel we were supposed to read for English Lit. I grudgingly picked it up and started to read. And then, a surprising thing happened. Shocking really. I actually started to like the book.

As I can remember, I hadn't read a book—at least on purpose or one I liked—in quite some time. What was strange was that I grew up loving to read. My mom read to me often, and I have fond memories of summers spent reading *The Hardy Boys* and *The Boxcar Children*. But somewhere along the line, like most teenagers perhaps, I traded in paperbacks for video games. But in that near-barren high school cafeteria on a spring Saturday morning, I began to rediscover my love for reading.

This passion has grown ever since. In college I was introduced to books that I loved in the genres of Christian living and theology. During my Master's Degree in England, I learned to read widely and read for the main idea. During my doctoral program, one of my favorite activities was reading from lists drafted by our lead mentor. There were books that I loved, others I didn't care for, and still others that made me downright mad. But they all grew and stretched me. One morning as I sat in my office surveying my bookshelves, I was reminded how much I've been shaped by people I have never met. I am convinced that I am a better leader, husband, father, friend, and follower of God through the books I have read.

New York Times bestselling author Michael Hyatt wrote a blog post on the secret to Dr. Ben Carson's success. Early on, the deck was stacked against Carson. He was raised in extreme poverty by a single mom in Detroit, Michigan. In an interview, Carson explained to Hyatt that while his mom was out working several jobs to support her family, she noticed "that wealthy people read a lot of books and didn't spend a lot of time watching television." So Ben's mom unplugged the television and sent her boys to the library. Their job was to read two books a week and submit a written report. It worked. "Within the space of a year and a half … [Carson] went from the bottom of the class to the top." In the interview, Hyatt said that for Carson, reading created new possibilities, gave him a sense that he had the power to change his future, and gave him a new self-confidence.[6]

Dr. Suess says it well:

*The more you read*
*The more things that you'll know*
*The more that you learn*
*The more places you'll go.*[7]

Need some inspiration? To get your child engaged with scripture, *The Jesus Storybook Bible* is one of the best Bibles for children I have ever seen. It not only tells the stories of scripture, but the story of scripture—as in the story of Jesus. The story of Christ and the gospel is found throughout.

For children who are around eight or older, I highly recommend *50 Things Every Young Gentleman Should Know* and for girls, *50 Things Every Young Lady Should Know.* I'll refrain from going on a rant about how many children today don't know basic manners and about their behavior (or lack thereof) in grocery stores and restaurants. But these books are a must! While good manners and behavior may not get your kids into heaven, they sure will make the journey there a lot more enjoyable!

---

Good manners and behavior may not get your kids into heaven, they sure will make the journey there a lot more enjoyable!

---

There are also faith-adventure books like *The Chronicles of Narnia, The Space Trilogy,* or the more recent series on the adventures of Jack Staples. However you choose to do it, read to your kids (and have them read on their own) early and often. Cultivating a love for reading within your children will expand their world and expand their faith.

3) Teach the Power of Being a Lifelong Learner

Recently I attended a birthday party. (Well, kind of.) On what would have been his 90th birthday, family and friends gathered in the auditorium of Epicenter Church in Fayetteville, NC to celebrate the life of Pastor (Dr.) Gardner Altman Sr. The memorial service for Pastor Altman was indeed a celebration. We heard story after story of the amazing impact of his life. The day culminated with the bestowing of the highest honor in NC, the Governor's Award, and declaring December 21 in Fayetteville to be "Gardner Altman Sr. Day", The service was followed by a "birthday party" to celebrate his life. Although the stories of his life would fill pages and pages, I'll share only one

When Pastor Altman was only twelve years old, he began selling produce in Raleigh, NC. Having a good business mind from a young age, he did well for himself. However, because of the job, sixth grade marked the end of his formal education. Years later, he fell in love and married, and a couple of years after that, at a camp meeting revival service, committed his life to Christ and felt a call to full-time ministry. Not wanting to be an uneducated minister, he set off to Southeastern University (at that time Southeastern Bible Institute) in Lakeland, FL. The only problem was most colleges would not take people who only had a sixth-grade education!

When Altman arrived on campus, his business mind immediately noticed that construction and buildings were going up. He went into the offices and began talking with the college leadership about the construction and the cost of such an endeavor. Then, as only a shrewd businessman could, he said, "Gentlemen, I'll tell you what.

I will write you a check for my first year's tuition up front. If after a year, I can't cut it, then you can dismiss me." They accepted his offer!

Young Gardner took college classes during the day. As amazing as that feat is in and of itself, he realized that he needed a high school education too. He also took high school classes at night. A few years later, he graduated with his college degree and high school diploma in the same year.

This posture as a lifelong learner was something Pastor Altman continued throughout his life. He attained postgraduate degrees from Southwestern Baptist Theological Seminary in Wake Forest and the Assemblies of God Theological Seminary in Springfield, MO, as well as completing graduate work at Duke University. He was an avid reader, believing that when you stop reading, you stop leading.

This love for learning was something he passed on to his children and grandchildren as well. One granddaughter commented that she remembers her grandfather stressing the importance of education, telling her that people may be able to take your money, but they can never take your mind.

I love this story because it emphasizes what has come to be an essential core value for my life: being a lifelong learner. Throughout my educational journey, one of the most important things I've learned is not necessarily the information itself, but the value of continual learning, reading, growing, and trying new things. When you graduate with a doctoral degree, it's referred to as a "terminal" degree, as in "end". I think that's the worst name ever. A degree, of any sort, isn't the end of learning; it's just the beginning.

---

A degree, of any sort, isn't the end of learning; it's just the beginning.

---

## FAITH AND COLLEGE

Before we leave the topic of education and the value of being a lifelong learner, I must say a word about college. The statistics are grim. Between 50-67 percent of kids who go to a secular college or university for three to four years end up leaving their faith. On the contrary, of students who attend a Christian college or university, 90 percent report growing in their faith.[8] Watching parents invest so much physically, mentally, emotionally, and spiritually in the lives of their children for 18 years to have it all wiped out in college is sad.

Parents, for me, I see really only two options. I believe the best option is a Christian college where students are in a culture surrounded by friends, professors, and mentors who will build them up and invest in their lives. However, if a secular university is in play, then they must immediately get plugged into a healthy college ministry such as Chi Alpha, Cru, FCA, or InterVarsity. If the college your child is attending doesn't have a thriving campus ministry, then I would check it off the list just as fast as though it didn't offer the major in which they were interested.

4) Have an *Oh, The Places You'll Go* Life

One of the things my wife and I have made a core value in our family is travel. We have chosen to live in a modest (paid-for) house and live on a budget well below our means. Because of these choices, we're able to put money into travel savings. My job includes travel and so we pick some periodic places for the entire family to go. So far, our kids have been blessed to see the Grand Canyon, hike mountains, see the fall foliage in quaint New Hampshire towns, ride the ferry to a remote island off the North Carolina coast, go ice skating in New York City, and visit other places as well. Travel is about helping them see, feel, and experience. I hope these experiences will fuel a sense of adventure throughout their lives.

Please hear me. Travel doesn't have to be far, and it doesn't have to be expensive! This isn't license for you to swipe your credit card and go on a cruise. When I was growing up, it was tent camping at Lake Erie. When I was a broke college student, it was sleeping in the car and eating peanut butter sandwiches with my buddies by the beach. Whatever your budget allows, pick fun adventures for your family to share.

Travel in and of itself is a wonderful gift. Travel with a faith element is even better. One of the best pieces of advice I could give any parent as it relates to seeing new lands is to send your child on a short-term missions trip. As a youth pastor, one of my goals was to take every student on a missions trip before he or she graduated from high school. I have taken both global and stateside trips to Colombia, El Salvador, Detroit, Atlanta, Honduras, Singapore, the Philippines, Ireland, Zambia, and Australia. One of my favorite experiences has been watching the eyes of students come alive with faith.

Recently, the idea of short-term trips has come under attack. *Isn't it basically just a vacation? Couldn't the money just be sent to the missionaries?* Both are a resounding "no!" First of all, if you've ever been on a missions trip, you know you've never worked so hard in all your life! Second, no experience compares to seeing firsthand how people in other countries live. When your child sleeps on a floor, eats rice and beans, holds an orphan in his or her arms, and prays for a woman and sees God heal her, these experiences are priceless. Also, kids who go on short-term trips today are tomorrow's leaders and givers in the church.

## JOSH

Josh is one of my students in a college course I'm teaching. He's studying for the ministry. He's an avid reader and thinker, but he's also fun-loving and adventurous. He's a volunteer youth leader at his church and spent the previous summer in Arizona teaching mountain biking at a Young Life camp. After he graduates, he plans to spend 90 days traveling to all 48 of the contiguous states.

As he was telling me about his plans, he also told me about his childhood. Some Fridays, his mom and dad would pick his sister and him up from school. Their bags were packed and his dad would say, "Pick a direction: north, east, south, or west." Then they would set out on an adventure. No plans. No map. No itinerary. Just a spontaneous trip.

Josh is one of those kids with an amazing sense of adventure. His eyes sparkle with possibility. He's a dreamer and a world changer. I asked how much of his sense of adventure came from those trips. "Oh, a lot," he said. As he continued talking about future plans, he described the moments when you return from a trip, show someone a picture of the place you've been, and find the photo doesn't do justice to the experience. He explained, "That's what I want my life to be filled with—experiences that cannot be put into words."

Josh's adventures aren't limited to his travels. He lives a faith-adventure as well. As a high school student, his youth pastor challenged the kids in the youth minister to look for people at school needing prayer. A couple of days later, after lunch in the cafeteria, he prayed with a friend who had a splitting headache. The friend was healed. Sometimes when you step out and believe that God can do anything, He does exactly that.

Josh lives a faith-adventure. David lived a faith-adventure. Your children can live a faith-adventure too. By cultivating God-given wonder, awe, and curiosity in your children, they grow up continuing to have faith in God, dream big dreams, and choose adventure.

## Group Discussion Guide

1) Of the four practical ways to implement faith-adventure in the lives of your child(ren) (listed below), which do you believe is your greatest strength? Which is your greatest weakness? How can you strengthen your weakest area and the others in between?
2) Discuss and create four faith-adventures for your child(ren).
   a. Keep asking questions
      Utilizing the scripture passage from Psalm 19:1, create an activity that encourages questions, i.e. a camping trip, outdoor movie environment, night time walk on the beach.
   b. Make reading Fun-damental
      What was your favorite book as a child? Why? Reread the book, then have your child(ren) read the same book. Have a discussion with them on why they liked/disliked the book. Look for similarities in your answers. Make room for laughter in the discussion. Then, do the same thing with the first passage of scripture you ever learned.
   c. Become a Lifelong-Learner
      What is a reasonable goal to set for intentional learning experiences/activities with your child(ren)? Discuss how every activity has the potential to be a learning activity. How can you encourage your child(ren) to become "addicted" to learning?
   d. Create an *Oh, The Places You'll Go* Life
      What was your favorite vacation as a child? Why? Have you ever been on a missions trip? How did that experience change or impact who you are today? Discuss how this type of life will fit into your family. Pull out a calendar and begin to dream about the places you will go and then turn them into a reality.

# 7

## A Child Who is Strong

*"Your servant has killed both the lion and the bear..."*

*(1 Samuel 17:36)*

Following a wildfire, horticulturists wanted to jump-start the regrowth process. They took sapling trees from a greenhouse and planted them in the areas destroyed by the fire. Almost all of them died. They were confused. The environment in which the trees were planted had good soil, sunshine, water, and almost no outside factors such as disease or weeds that would overtake them. Why didn't they survive? The horticulturists discovered the problem was that the trees were raised in a greenhouse. They grew up in an ecosystem where they were coddled, protected, and where everything was provided for them. While this setting may have made for a comfortable beginning to their lives, they couldn't survive in the real world.[1]

That's tough to hear, isn't it? Part of our parental instinct is to nurture, protect, and provide, and those are all good and Godly things. But when we overdo it, we can end up hindering our children.

## A Lesson from Some Runners

Christopher McDougall has written a fascinating book on the Tarahumara Indians, a tribe living among the cliffs of the Copper Creek Canyon in Mexico.[2] Basically, they are a tribe of super athletes. Little to no disease exists among the tribe. There is no obesity, no high blood pressure, and no depression. And they can easily run fifty miles a day. At age 80. Barefoot. Running injuries? They're unheard of.

Contrast this fact with the number of running injuries in America, which are especially high in recent times. In fact, 1972, brought a documented spike in the number of running injuries. What happened in 1972 that caused this dramatic increase? This year marked the emergence of a small athletic company out of the University of Oregon called Nike. Lest you think this correlation is a coincidence, physicians explain the connection. If you look at an average running shoe, where do you find the most cushioning, padding, and support? It is in the arch and the heel. (Think Nike "Air" or "Shox".) The thought behind the design of these shoes was that they provide a layer of support for your arch and cushioning for your heel.

This design has a couple of problems. First, an arch, by its very nature, is engineered to support itself. Think of an archway in a large building, or the entrance to a train tunnel. If this archway had columns beneath it, you would think it to be strange. Architecturally, an arch is one of the strongest parts of a building. Likewise, the arch of your foot is designed to be strong and to self-supportive. When you support something that doesn't need support, you weaken the structure.

Second, the layer of cushioning designed to protect your heel actually causes you to run incorrectly. If you were to run barefoot across the lawn on a cool summer morning, your heel wouldn't touch the ground, because if it did, it would hurt. Your body instinctively does things the right way. But when you add a layer of cushioning to your heel, heel-to-toe running no longer hurts, so your body adapts and begins to run incorrectly, causing injury.

The results of both issues are not good. Think of it this way. After the removal of a cast on your arm, you will find that your muscles have atrophied. What was once strong and vibrant is now withered and weak. The same thing happens when you wear overly cushioned and supportive shoes. You are essentially wearing a cast on your foot. God designed your foot to be self-supporting and strong. When you wrap it in artificial protection, it becomes weak.

Parents, do you hear the message? When we add cushioning and support to things that are designed to be strong, we only serve to weaken them. Please hear this: Your kids are strong. God made them that way. They are stronger than you think. They are tougher than you think. Every time you come to their rescue, you are not strengthening them; you are weakening them.

---

When we add cushioning and support to things that are designed to be strong, we only serve to weaken them.

---

## Move Over Helicopter, Here Comes the Lawnmower

At the beginning of the book, we talked about helicopter parents—parents who hover, cover, and smother, all in the name of wanting what's best for their child. Columnist Bryan Greeson says that the apt metaphor is no longer helicopters, but lawnmowers. Greeson describes chatting with a teacher and mentioning something about helicopter parents. The teacher responded, "Oh no, Bryan, that's not the latest. We are now seeing lawnmower parents. They don't just hover over their kids—they walk in front of them for everything that may be in the way and cut a clear, smooth path."[3]

What are they mowing? You may be surprised. The clearing goes far beyond helping a little too much with their fifth grader's science project. Over-involvement is extending to college, and beyond. Parents are filling out their children's college applications, emailing the professor if Johnny College Boy gets a bad grade, and even writing papers for them. I've read reports of parents calling their adult child's boss at work if they feel their child isn't treated fairly.

The headmaster at our kids' school is a great friend of mine. He tells the story of being sent home from school as a boy with a sign hung around his neck that read, "I can't stop talking." He got paddled twice—once from his mother for talking, and once from his father for not being smart enough to take the sign off before he got home.

Imagine what would happen today. The parent would immediately place a phone call to the principal. "How dare the teacher embarrass my child like that!" Mom and dad would coddle the child to make sure his or her feelings weren't hurt. The local news would surely get hold of the story, and might even be a lawsuit for defamation of character. But every time parents undercut the authority structure in their children's lives and bail them out, they teach them disrespect for authority and weaken their children.

## Marshmallow Children

A now-famous study in psychology has come to be known simply as "The Marshmallow Test." Researchers placed preschool children in a room with a single marshmallow. The kids were told they could eat the marshmallow whenever they wanted. However, the researcher told the kids that he or she was going to leave the room, and if the child waited until the researcher came back, they could have two marshmallows. When the researchers followed up on these children fifteen years later, the results were astounding. The children who were able to exhibit self-control and defer gratification at an early age were found to be more successful, to have better marriages, to have better health, and to be making more money.

Since the initial experiment in the 1960's, researchers have examined the findings from different angles. One of the offshoot studies involved testing the effect overprotective, controlling parents have on their children. The test proceeded as follows: A child was allowed to play in a room with his or her parent. The parent was taken out of the room to see how the child would cope with separation from the parent. After this part of the experiment, the child went through the marshmallow test. What effect, if any, did the child's ability to cope with separation from his or her parent have on his or her ability to maintain self-control during the marshmallow test? Researchers discovered that the kids who were able to separate themselves from Mom and Dad during the together playtime were able to cope exceedingly better when the parent left. Furthermore, they demonstrated much higher levels of self-control during the marshmallow test.[4] In other words, the less "helicoptering" by the parent, the more self-assured the child turned out to be.

The less "helicoptering" by the parent, the more self-assured the child turned out to be.

## The Lion and the Bear

Turning back to our story of young David, I love the credentials that he gives when trying to convince Saul to give him a shot at fighting Goliath. All of the trained soldiers are scared and hiding. But

David, with confidence in his God, volunteers to slay the giant. Of course, as with many situations where someone attempts greatness in the presence of cowards, the fear-filled will do their best to pull the courageous back down to their level of mediocrity. They taunt and mock David. Who does he think he is? What makes him think that he could defeat this gigantic, well-trained warrior? You've got to love David's reply:

> "Your servant has been keeping his father's sheep. When a lion or a bear came and carried off a sheep from the flock, I went after it, struck it and rescued the sheep from its mouth. When it turned on me, I seized it by its hair, struck it and killed it. Your servant has killed both the lion and the bear; this uncircumcised Philistine will be like one of them, because he has defied the armies of the living God. The Lord who rescued me from the paw of the lion and the paw of the bear will rescue me from the hand of this Philistine" (1 Samuel 17:34-37).

Basically, David says, "I know God can use me to kill Goliath, because I've already killed a lion and a bear." Wait. What? A teenage kid has already taken down two of the fiercest animals on the planet? If, as some scholars believe, David was only fifteen when he killed Goliath, then he was even younger that that when he went all Crocodile Hunter on a lion and bear in the wild.[5] In other words, because David was not hovered over and kept "safe" in the house and was allowed to develop toughness in the wilderness of the field, he was able to defeat Goliath.

Following Jesus is a risk-filled life. Our kids don't need a childhood that is safe from risk. They need a childhood where it is safe to risk.[6] Lions and bears are necessary training grounds for giant killers.

Sometimes it seems we would rather raise our kids in arenas where we have taken the teeth out of the lions and declawed the bears.

---

Following Jesus is a risk-filled life. Our kids don't need a childhood that is safe from risk. They need a childhood where it is safe to risk.

---

So, yes, we need to allow our kids to face tough things. But if we're not careful, we can miss a key connection in this passage. Notice that David is not just facing lions and bears for the sake of facing lions and bears. He's not doing hard things just for the sake of struggle. David makes it clear that he is acutely aware it was, "The Lord who rescued me from the paw of the lion and the paw of the bear." There is connection between struggle and a cultivation of the awareness of the Presence of God.

Have you not found connection to be true in your own life? Think back to a particularly difficult time in your own life—the loss of a close friend or relative, the loss of a job, or an unexpected move. Despite the difficulty of going through this time, in hindsight, what sustained you? Later on when he was running for his life from King Saul, David wrote, "The Lord is near to the broken-hearted."[7] Isn't it often during our greatest struggles that we learn our greatest dependence upon God and cultivate an even more acute awareness of Jesus' presence in our lives?

One of the greatest gifts we can give our children is to fly the helicopter back to the landing pad, put the lawnmower back in the garage, and allow our kids to face tough situations. We can back away because we're not leaving them alone; we're leaving them in the hands of Someone greater! Yes, it will build grit and character. But, most importantly, it teaches them to draw near to Jesus and the power of the Holy Spirit.

---

One of the greatest gifts we can give our children is to fly the helicopter back to the landing pad, put the lawnmower back in the garage, and allow our kids to face tough situations. We can back away because we're not leaving them alone; we're leaving them in the hands of Someone greater!

---

## The Blessing of a Skinned Knee (Kids Need to Fail)

The title of New York Times bestselling author, Wendy Mogul's book says it all. Today's children desperately need *The Blessing of a Skinned Knee.*[8] Dr. Mogel owned a successful counseling practice in a beautiful part of Southern California. While counseling family after family, child after child, she began to feel disconnected from her own family. She took a year off, which sent her on a journey of faith of rediscovering her Jewish roots. One of the things Mogul realized along the way was that the vast majority of parents she counseled were trying to preemptively rescue their kids from all types of hardship. She emerged with a newfound wholeness and a determination to parent her own children differently and to teach other parents how to do the same.

Dr. Mogul says that "the current trend in parenting is to shield children from emotional or physical discomfort."[9] This trend is destroying our kids. Mogul says that we are raising our children like we're cruise ship directors and that our goal has somehow become to get them to adulthood without the slightest bump or wave. She writes, "They are trying to inoculate their children against the pain of life. There is a Hebrew phrase, *tzar gidul banim,* that refers to ... our own children's pain. Without it they cannot grow strong. They won't learn to swim."[10] Our kids need to encounter life and encounter God on their own.

Let's be clear: the Bible teaches that God is not the cause of hardship and trial. Those things are the result of Satan and sin, the enemy and a fallen world. However, God wants to redeem our tough circumstances by using them to toughen us up. Paul tells us, "We also glory in our sufferings, because we know that suffering produces perseverance; perseverance, character; and character, hope.[11] When we try at all costs to keep hurt and failure away from our kids, what if we're really keeping away the very circumstances God wants to use to produce greater fruit in their lives?

As a parent, this approach can be hard. In some ways, we're wired to put on our cape and come to the rescue. If our child is struggling to make new friends on the playground, we want to come to the rescue. If our child is struggling in algebra, we want to come to the rescue. Watching our kids fall can be one of the toughest things as a parent. Allowing them to walk through painful situations seems to go against our very instincts. But remember that in our rush to put a Band-Aid on everything in life, those Band-Aids eventually become casts.

In our rush to put a Band-Aid on everything in life, those Band-Aids eventually become casts.

## Growing Wings (Kids Need to Struggle)

My daughter Ana loves butterflies. And bugs. And caterpillars. And frogs. What's funny is that she is also loves princesses, ballet, and painted nails. It is not unusual to see Ana out in the yard in a pink tutu, covered in dirt, and carrying a toad. Because of her love of butterflies, we took a few caterpillars and placed them in a glass jar. We punched holes in the top for air and put some sticks and leaves in there for food. We enjoyed watching the transformation process from caterpillar to cocoon to butterfly.

The butterfly's wings are formed in a cocoon. You probably knew that. But what you may not have known is that the pressure of the cocoon is crucial to the wing formation process. If you were to watch a butterfly as it "struggles" to emerge from the cocoon, you might think, "Oh, that poor butterfly is struggling. I'll help out by assisting it out of the cocoon." If you did that, the result would be a butterfly that's unable to fly. That final struggle out of the cocoon is crucial to the wing formation process. In the struggle, under pressure, the butterfly's wings gain the final growth and strength to enable flight.[12]

Too many times parents think they're "helping". "Helping" by doing too much of a homework assignment. "Helping" by rushing in and calling a friend's parent to resolve a conflict between the kids. "Helping" by calling the teacher because their kid got a C. When we preemptively rescue our children, either from the consequences of their actions or by not allowing them to problem-solve on their own, we clip their wings and short-circuit their purpose. Perhaps the question for us is: Do we have the faith to allow our children to develop their faith?

## The Power of "Yet" (Kids Need to Develop Determination)

Carol Dweck has written a fascinating book entitled *Mindset,* where she tackles the question, "What is the difference between successful and unsuccessful people?" In all of her research, she came to the following conclusion: the difference between people who succeed in life and those who don't, has very little to do with natural talent or ability. This critical factor all comes down to: did they have a fixed mindset, or a growth mindset? People with a fixed mindset tend to believe they are destined to live with whatever life deals them, and they have a fixed amount of talent, ability, and resources. If they fail at something, they assume they aren't going to transcend that failure. On the other hand, people with a growth mindset tend to believe failure isn't final. Failure may have been an event, but it doesn't define them. Get knocked down seven, get up eight. These individuals, time and time again, outperform others, even people who may have more "natural" talent and ability.[13]

If you have seen the movie *Moneyball,* you are familiar with Billy Beane. Billy was the general manager of the Oakland A's who implemented a new strategy for winning baseball based more on algorithms for compiling the right players than stockpiling the most talented (and highest paid) players. He succeeded in winning 103 games that season—with the second lowest payroll in baseball.

What many people may not know is Billy's back story. Growing up, Beane was an incredibly gifted natural athlete. People were calling him the next Babe Ruth. He excelled in just about everything he did. By the time he was a sophomore in high school, he was the leading scorer on the basketball team, the quarterback of the football team, and batted .500 on the baseball team. But all of that talent never translated into success at the Major League level.

While Billy had all the talent in the world, he never learned how to handle failure. It was said about him that, "It wasn't merely that he didn't like to fail; it was if he didn't know how to fail." When he struck out, he would look for something to break. He was a perfectionist, thinking that he should never make an out. He couldn't handle failure and never looked to fix the problem. His fixed mindset led to the demise of his playing career.

Contrast Billy Beane to another player who came up through the minor leagues at the same time and was Beane's teammate with the Philadelphia Phillies. Lenny Dykstra was the classic overachiever. While Dykstra was not born with the same level of natural ability, he had a growth mindset. He was a scrappy player. Nobody was going to outwork or outhustle him. (His nickname was "Nails," if that tells you anything.) To see him play was oftentimes to see the front of his uniform covered in dirt from a headfirst slide into a base or diving to catch a ball. As Beane himself said of Dykstra, "He had no concept of failure." Lenny ended up being a three-time All-Star and a World Series Champion.

We must understand the power of the growth (vs. fixed) mindset in raising our children. Turns out that it's not about your child's natural ability, but about developing a growth mindset. When we helicopter parent, we raise kids who don't know how to handle failure. And kids who don't know how to fail end up not knowing how to succeed.[14]

---

Kids who don't know how to fail end up not knowing how to succeed.

---

## From "Growth Mindset" to "Grow-in-Faith" Mindset

For Christian kids, a "growth mindset" is good, but a "grow-in-faith" mindset is even better! With Jesus, every failure becomes a chance to learn and every fall an opportunity to find comfort in Christ. Furthermore, for us who are raising kids who love Jesus, failure provides a great opportunity to teach a powerful theological truth—*Cristus Victor.* For the first thousand years of the church, *Cristus Victor* was the predominant theology of Christian life—Jesus defeated and disarmed the powers of darkness on the cross, was resurrected from the grave, is seated triumphantly at the right hand of the Father, and fills us with this very same resurrection power to live victoriously through Christ. Keep in mind these were the very same Christians who were being hunted down and killed for their faith. Even when we lose, we win!

> With Jesus, every failure becomes a chance to learn and every fall an opportunity to find comfort in Christ.

As the Apostle Paul reminds us, "In all these things we are more than conquerors through him who loved us. For I am convinced that neither death nor life, neither angels nor demons, neither the present nor the future, nor any powers, neither height nor depth, nor anything else in all creation, will be able to separate us from the love of God that is in Christ Jesus our Lord."[15] Struggle is not just for the sake of struggle. Struggle should draw us closer to Christ.

What we need to remember as Christian parents is that we are not just raising our kids to be "tough" for the sake of being tough. It's about so much more than just teaching them grit and determination. This is about lions and bears and giants. There are some pretty big giants in this world. There are systems and structures and sins that daily defy the people of God and the message of the gospel. They come out with daily taunts against Christ and His church. But through the resurrection power of Christ, God wants our children to take on those things and emerge victorious.

## Fourth Person in the Fire

One of my favorite parts of the story of Shadrach, Mesach, and Abednigo, the three Hebrew teenagers who were thrown into the fiery furnace because of their refusal to succumb to peer pressure and bow to anything other than their God, is that when the soldiers looked in the furnace, they exclaimed, "There is a fourth person in the fire, and he looks like the son of God."[16] Some theologians believe this is a pre-incarnate appearance of Christ. They weren't just in the fire. They were in the fire with Jesus.

Parents, isn't that great to know? When our kids are going through the fire, they aren't alone. Jesus himself is with them. He has promised never to leave them or forsake them.

When our kids are going through the fire, they aren't alone. Jesus himself is with them. He has promised never to leave them or forsake them.

This was true for David as well. He didn't just face a lion and a bear. He knew the Lord had "rescued me from the paw of the lion and the paw of the bear" and because of that past history, he knew God would also "rescue me from the hand of this Philistine." David didn't just learn to fight battles; he learned to recognize the Presence of God in the midst of his battles.

David is named as the author of 75 Psalms. Many of those Psalms reference the Presence of God. I'm convinced that one of the reasons David was so close to the Lord was because of those years in the field. Yes, I'm sure there were sweet moments of prayer and worship underneath the stars where he sensed God was near. But I also believe it was in lion-and-bear times where David cultivated a deep awareness of God's Presence.

## Das Kitafahrten

A recent article in The Wall Street Journal began, "Tilda Geyer got away from her parents on a trip to a lake last summer. She and 10 friends slept in tents, rode horses, picked berries, and flew on a rope swing over the water. At night, they sang around a campfire." She was four. The campout was for kindergarteners. There were no parents, and adult supervision was minimal.[17]

I'm smiling as I write, because if this scenario occurred in most schools in the U.S., parents would either be in a rage or a panic. Can you imagine if your kindergartener came home with a permission slip for a field trip to the forest? But this approach is the conviction of German kindergartens. The fundamental philosophy of German educators is that children are tough and will not only survive in this type of environment, but will actually have fun and thrive. On these trips, the kids learn to use knives, whittle their own sticks, and roast bratwurst over an open fire. They aren't put at risk for injury or death, but rather minimal supervision provides an atmosphere of exploration and learning. They learn to figure out problems for themselves or work together with other kids, rather than having an adult do everything for them.

In America, we think our kids need to be coddled and cuddled. In other parts of the world, the belief is that children need to be challenged and empowered. The philosophy finds its origin in the very roots of "kindergarten" or "Child Garden". Kindergarten, as 19th-century German educator and founder Friedrich Fröbel envisioned it, was intended to set kids free in nature, where they could learn from everyday experiences. To this day, many German kids learn to rough it in the woods before they learn to read, some even before they are fully potty trained. So maybe we should ask Bear Grylls (of *Man vs. Wild* fame) to become a kindergarten teacher.

## Leaping onto the Basketball Court

My dad taught me so many things. Being tough was one of them. Toughness is kind of in our blood. Growing up in western PA, we're Steelers fans. The Steelers are tough, and Steelers fans are tough. The

Steelers defense in the 1970's was nicknamed "The Steel Curtain". They had players like "Mean" Joe Greene, Jack Lambert (the middle linebacker with two missing front teeth), and cornerback Mel Blount. (The NFL literally changed the rules because Blount was too tough for receivers to handle.) One of their chief rivals during this era was the Dallas Cowboys. The Cowboys were known as "America's Team." The Cowboys had all the glitz and glamour. The Cowboys had cheerleaders. The Steelers had grit.

As tough as my dad was, he was usually pretty calm about it. He didn't let his emotions get out of control. That's why I was surprised when, after one of my brother's basketball games, with about two leaps, he came bounding out of the bleachers and leapt onto the court.

My brother Steve was in a basketball tournament in 6th grade. He was the star of the team and was scoring at will in the first half. At halftime, the coach on the other team made an adjustment and began to double-team my brother. Our team wasn't ready for this defense and never made an adjustment. The other team came back to win. I don't remember all of the circumstances, but I do know that our coach wasn't happy with the refs. In a kind of protest after the game, instead of lining up to shake hands with the other team, our team headed straight for the locker room.

That's when Dad cleared a tall building in a single bound.

Two leaps out of the bleachers and a dash across the basketball court, and our team was headed back out onto the court, walking over to the other team to shake hands and congratulate them.

Dad wasn't mad at our coach for failing to make an offensive adjustment. He wasn't mad at the refs or the other team. He didn't yell at his own kid for failing to dribble through the double-team. The only thing that made his blood boil was a lack of sportsmanship and character. The only thing my dad was concerned about "rescuing" these kids from was a bad attitude.

## Letting Go

One of my best friends in ministry is Dale Jenkins. He and I served as youth pastors together in the same town. He took the lead pastor position at the same church, and our friendship grew throughout the years. One morning, I was scrolling through Twitter and came across a blog post from Dale. He and his wife Carrie had just taken their firstborn daughter, Gabby, to college and dropped her off. As the father of a little girl, I'm a sucker for anything daddy-daughter related, and this post was no different. It moved me to tears as Dale wrote about the experience of dropping off Gabby:

> Yesterday we moved our daughter into her college dorm.
>
> Over 4,000 freshmen are attending Liberty University this fall, and they all moved into their dorms on the same day! Traffic was bumper to bumper over the entire campus, but the Liberty Student-Leaders were stationed to direct traffic, answer questions, and even to carry all of the luggage! They made the process so easy.
>
> We spent several hours working on Gabby's room—unpacking her boxes, organizing her clothes, rearranging the room, making her bed, etc. Her roommate is wonderful, and Gabby also knows a couple of other people on campus.
>
> Carrie (my incredible and beautiful wife) and Gabby had done such a great job thinking through the details before the move. In fact, that afternoon we ended up only having to do a quick run for a few items. After a wonderful dinner with friends, we returned to the dorm, and soon the finishing touches were complete.
>
> Saying goodbye was not as difficult as I thought it would be, perhaps because we were all so busy doing things and keeping our minds on what was practical. Or perhaps because

it was getting late and we were all a bit tired. Or perhaps it was because there is such a peace in our hearts, knowing that Gabby is exactly where God wants her to be. I couldn't be any more proud of her. She is so ready for this new season of life.

The drive home was made easy by the great conversation. Carrie and I were so glad that one of our spiritual daughters—Krysta—made the trip with us. We even got to talk with Gabby on the phone before she went to bed. She was doing great.

This morning I rose early and immediately missed my girl. I am fighting tears as I write these words.

Funny how you can experience sorrow and joy all at the same time.

Jesus said that life would be like that—momentary sorrow, everlasting joy.

Jesus said, "A little while and you will not see me, and again a little while and you will see me? Truly, truly, I say to you, you will weep and lament, but the world will rejoice. You will be sorrowful, but your sorrow will turn into joy. When a woman is giving birth, she has sorrow because her hour has come, but when she has delivered the baby, she no longer remembers the anguish, for joy that a human being has been born into the world. So also you have sorrow now, but I will see you again, and your hearts will rejoice, and no one will take your joy from you. In that day you will ask nothing of me. Truly, truly, I say to you, whatever you ask of the Father in my name, he will give it to you. Until now you have asked nothing in my name. Ask, and you will receive, that your joy may be full" (John 16:19-24 ESV).

Why would we want to endure the "sorrow" of being away from our girl? Because there is a greater joy in knowing

> that she is growing, learning, and experiencing all that God has planned for her life!
>
> The joy far outweighs the sorrow, and it certainly will outlast it!
>
> Father, today I pray for parents who are sending their kids off—whether it is to kindergarten or college, marriage or the mission field. Help us to rest in your peace and to receive the everlasting joy of knowing that "all of our children shall be taught of The Lord, and great shall be the peace of our children."[18]

What a powerful image! This father understands that even through tears, he is releasing his daughter into God's purpose. Moms and dads, this is a great goal to parent toward. When your son or daughter begins college, hopefully you will get a text that says something like, "I miss you mom. I miss you dad. But I'm ready to go change the world."

## Releasing

John's account of the resurrection includes an encounter with Mary in the garden. Mary was at the tomb and had seen it was empty. Thinking someone had stolen the body of her Lord, she begins to cry. Turning, she sees someone standing there who she mistook for the gardener. When the gardener says her name, "Mary!" she recognizes him to be Jesus. Apparently Mary then reaches out to grasp hold of Jesus, because He says to her, "Don't cling to me, for I haven't yet ascended to the Father."[19]

Translation: The activity of the risen Christ in your life is too big to contain or control.

Translation: What you try to cling to, you lose.

Translation: What God is trying to do in the life of your child is bigger than you. If you try to hold on too tightly, you'll stifle it.

---

The activity of the risen Christ in your life is too big to contain or control. What God is trying to do in the life of your child is bigger than you. If you try to hold on too tightly, you'll stifle it.

---

The things that are truly grandiose and spectacular in life, you can't hold onto.

Can you grasp an ocean wave?

Can you cling to a sunset?

I know that you gave birth to them (or were at least there for their birth). I know you held them and fed them. I know you buckled them into car seats. I know you picked them up when they skinned their knee and dried their tears. I know you consoled them when someone broke their heart. I know they carry your last name. But they don't belong to you. You only steward them for the King. The Hebrew language doesn't even a verb for possession. *Yesh li*, which we sometimes translate "to have" literally means "it is there for me."[20] Parents:

Your child is not your trophy.
Your child is not your *magnum opus.* [21]
Your child isn't even yours.
He or she is the Lord's.

## Palms Up

I attended a conference recently where the speaker encouraged us to physically take the posture of a steward, with the understanding that we don't own anything, but rather steward everything as a resource of the King. He encouraged us to pray with our palms up. You would think that would be a fairly easy thing to do, but for this OCD, first-born, it was a challenge. There's something about physically holding your hands with your palms up that makes you realize that you're not in control. You're not an owner. Once you fight through the emotions of not having control, this posture is actually quite freeing.

Things that you try to grasp can get heavy. An owner shoulders responsibility. When you don't control it, you no longer carry the weight. A steward transfers the weight of raising children to the shoulders of Jesus. A steward enjoys the ride. A steward lives "palms up".

I encourage you to turn your palms up now as you as you pray this prayer out loud. (If you're on an airplane, I give you permission to wait until you're alone because if not, the person beside you is going to think that you're weirder than they already do.)

*I do not own anything. I am a steward. I do not own my children. They are yours, Lord. I steward them for your purposes and your glory. Because you are a good and kind and loving owner, you allow me to enjoy them along the way. I give them back to you to be used for your highest purposes and their highest potential.*

---

An owner shoulders responsibility. A steward transfers the weight of raising children to the shoulders of Jesus.

---

## FROM "KEEP THEM SAFE" TO "MAKE THEM DANGEROUS"

As parents, we have a "protective gene" inherent in us. We want our children to be safe. Part of that sense is natural and good. But as we learn the power of living "palms up" and releasing our children to the Lord, our focus needs to change. Author Erwin McManus tells the story of praying for his son before he went to sleep. He found himself praying the typical parent prayer of "Lord, keep him safe." In that moment, he stopped and found himself convicted. He changed his prayer to, "Lord, make him dangerous."

> May the Lord make our kids dangerous—dangerous to the enemy of our souls!
> May they be filled with courage.
> May they kill lions and bears.

This generation has giant killer in them, but they need to be trained in lion-and-bear battlegrounds. A generation won't do great things for God when they're older if they were never allowed to do hard things when they were younger. At some point, your children will encounter Goliath. The moment for them to summon courage, have faith in God, defeat the giant, and step into their purpose will arise. In that moment, will they have the fortitude to pick up the sling and stone? It depends. Were they allowed to kill a lion and a bear?

## Group Discussion Guide

1) Discuss ways you may have become a helicopter/lawnmower parent without realizing it. After evaluation, how has this type of parenting affected your child(ren)? How can you make positive steps of correction in this area?
2) Talk about a time in your life when you faced a really tough situation. How did it shape who you are? How, in hindsight, did God show himself faithful in and through that situation?
3) What are some instances where it was really tough for you to watch your child(ren) face a difficult situation? What were the outcomes? How did you find God faithful in these situations? Revisit some of these situations in a family discussion to discuss God's faithfulness in your lives and how He is strengthening you through them.
4) Pray both the "Palms Up" and the "Make Them Dangerous" prayers. Ask God to give you and your child(ren) opportunities to trust Him in these areas in order to strengthen you and your child(ren). Discuss the outcomes with your group.

# 8

## A Child Who is Courageous

*As Goliath moved closer to attack, David quickly ran out to meet him.*

*(1 Samuel 17:48).*

On April 15, 2013 at 2:49 pm as runners were nearing the finishing line in Boston, two pressure cooker bombs exploded. Understandably, most people ran away from the explosions. A few heroes ran toward them. One of those was Dr. Natalie Stavas. After running the Boston Marathon on a broken foot, Stavas raced to save as many lives as possible. As Stavas and her radiologist dad, Joe, neared the finish line after running a grueling 26.2 miles, the pair hear the blasts and immediately dove into the carnage to help. The 32-year-old physician, who's a pediatric resident at Boston Medical

Center, jumped over the barricades and started tending to the most severe cases. In doing so, Stavas provided lifesaving treatment to a number of seriously injured victims.

This scene is a picture of how the world operates. The majority run away from problems, but a few heroes run toward them. Perhaps nothing depicts this inclination better than the contrast of the Israelites and David. The two verses of scripture we're going to explore in this chapter are only separated grammatically by a few short paragraphs, but in reality, they're worlds apart. They serve as vivid descriptors of the difference between David and the rest of the Israelites.

The scene is that Goliath comes out and shouts his usual defiance—threats aimed at producing fear and insecurity in the people of God. The scriptures show us the two completely opposite responses:

> *Whenever the Israelites saw the man, they all fled from him in great fear.*[1]
>
> *As the Philistine moved closer to attack him, David ran quickly toward the battle line to meet him.*[2]

The Israelites were full of fear and ran away from their problems.

David was full of courage and ran toward his purpose.

This begs the question, will we raise children who run from things? Or toward things?

---

The Israelites were full of fear and ran away from their problems. David was full of courage and ran toward his purpose. This begs the question, will we raise children who run from things? Or toward things?

---

Out of all the amazing verses that describe young David, this one is probably my favorite. He ran toward the very thing that everyone else was running from. He didn't sneak up on Goliath. He didn't reluctantly inch up to Goliath. David's fast moving feet were a declaration of his faith. He made an, "I'm all in!" statement. David wasn't just running toward the giant, he was running toward his God and running toward his future. I want that for my kids. I want them never to run from challenges, but to run toward their dreams. Let's dive in and see how to raise children who don't run away from their fears but instead run with courage towards their God-given purpose. Here are six things that both David, and our kids, can run toward:

## Run Toward the Real Enemy

Notice that David makes a choice to run toward the real enemy—Goliath. *Well, of course he does. Isn't it obvious that Goliath is the enemy?* You would certainly think so. But remember that young, faith-filled David has just taken a verbal lashing from his brothers. They have hurled false accusations at him. They have demeaned him and put him down in front of others. You can see how David may be tempted to turn his "fight" away from Goliath and start fighting against his brothers.

One of the crucial aspects of life is to always remember who the real enemy is.

One of the crucial aspects of life is to always remember who the real enemy is.

Our environment of competition and comparison in which we live in will do its best to turn us and our kids toward a world of self-destructive rivalry. If we're not careful, we'll spend our time and energy fighting the wrong enemy.

We hear horror stories of this very thing on the news. Remember the Olympic ice-skater's husband who hired someone to take a pipe wrench to the kneecap of the competition so his wife will have a better chance of winning a medal? Or perhaps you heard the story of a mom who put a substance into the drinks of her son's teammates so they would be sick and her son could get more playing time.

Extreme stories? Of course. But isn't there some of this unhealthy competition and comparison that arises in us too? Hoping the other kid on your son's baseball team won't do as well so your kid can start at a certain position. Wanting to trample the other soccer team because their coach is obnoxious. Wanting your daughter to do better in gymnastics than her rival on her own team. The spirit of competition and comparison is destroying the ecosystem of childhood, turning parents into stressed-out generals, and childhood into a war zone.

*So, what are you arguing for? Going further down the road of "every kid gets a trophy"?* No. That's unrealistic. And that's not real life. But, like David, we have to remember who the real enemy is. Jesus reminds us, "Do not be afraid of those who kill the body but cannot kill the soul. Rather, be afraid of the One who can destroy both soul and body in hell."[3]

The real enemy is the enemy of our soul. He is out to steal, kill, and destroy. Through lies and deception, he is robbing people around us of real life in Jesus Christ. So yes, we have a battle to fight. But when the enemy can get us distracted through fighting each other, he distracts us from fighting enemies of poverty, disease, and racism. The real battle is the battle against injustice.

As my friend and leader of the national youth ministry of the Assemblies of God, Heath Adamson says, "To preach a gospel that does not include help for the poor and downtrodden is to preach a gospel that Jesus never preached. But to only preach a gospel of social justice is simply to offer people a better brand of eternal misery." Social justice is so important. But social justice without Jesus isn't the gospel. As the people of God, we should be at the forefront of standing for human rights. But *the* human right is that every man, woman, and child on planet Earth has a right to hear the gospel of Jesus.[4]

Let's teach our children to fight the injustice of bullying by standing up for others who are weaker than us. Let's teach our children to fight injustice by eating lunch with and including in their circle of friends kids who may be slower, different, or lonely. Let's teach our kids to fight injustice by giving to the poor and feeding the hungry. And let's teach our kids to fight the greatest injustice of all by sharing the light and life of Jesus Christ with those who don't know him yet.

## Run Toward Your Fears

The opening scene of *The Last Battle,* the last installment in C.S. Lewis' *The Chronicles of Narnia* series, begins with the story of Shift and Puzzle.[5] Shift is an old, conniving, manipulative ape and Puzzle is a rather simple minded donkey. One day Shift and Puzzle are walking near Caldron Pool, a place where a large waterfall empties into a pool below. From a distance, they see something floating in the pool. As they draw nearer, they see that it is the carcass of a lion. They devise that a hunter must have killed the lion upstream, taken the hide off of the lion, and thrown it into the water.

Because the water is cold and churning quite rapidly from the power of the waterfall, Shift doesn't want to go in to retrieve the hide. He manipulates Puzzle into doing the work and bringing the carcass out on land. Shift then has an idea. No one has seen Aslan (the lion who serve as the Christ-figure of Lewis' books) in quite some time.

So Shift decides to take the hide and, again through his manipulative ways, convince Puzzle to wear it as a disguise. Then, in the shadows of dusk and along the edges of the bushes, Shift begins to parade the "lion" around to the people of Narnia. He throws his voice and convinces the Narnians that this figure is Aslan. He begins to take control of the people through fear and deception.

The enemy has always attempted to rule through fear and deception.

The scriptures tell us that the enemy prowls around *like* a roaring lion,[6] but that Jesus *is* the Lion of Judah.[7] The Lion of Judah's roar is a roar of victory. The roar of the True Lion instills fear in the enemy and faith in the people of God. When the Lion of Judah roars, He fills us with his power and courage. Our children live in the roar of Christ, so that they can have the bravery to face their fears.

Goliath was roaring. He sent the Israelites running, but David heard the roar of his God over the roar of fear. The true roar of Christ will always expose the lies and deception of the enemy that manifest themselves as fears in the lives of our kids.

---

The enemy prowls around *like* a roaring lion, but Jesus *is* the Lion of Judah. We must hear the roar of our God over the roar of our fears.

---

## False Evidence Appearing Real

Fear isn't real. It's not. It's **F**alse **E**vidence **A**ppearing **R**eal. Even Scooby Doo knows that. Well, ok, he doesn't, but he should. Because the same thing happens to him every single episode, and he keeps falling for it.

During my senior year in college, my brother Steve, best friend Kevin, and I watched two shows almost every single afternoon. I won't tell you what the first one was because I'm kind of embarrassed about it, but I'll give you a hint: it ends in "90210". The other show was Scooby Doo. I'm not sure why we watched it every day because really there is only one episode of Scooby Doo. The storyline may include a different monster, but it's basically the same every time.

For those of you who aren't familiar with Scooby, or who may need a refresher, basically the story goes something like this: Fred, Daphne, Velma, Shaggy, and Scooby are driving along in the Mystery Machine. Apparently they need a good mechanic, because it is always breaking down. And does it break down in front of a Sheetz, QT, or WaWa where they can go inside for a snack and call a tow truck? Of course not. It breaks down in front of the abandoned carnival. The only person on the premises is the janitor, Mr. Smithers. He tells the kids that just a couple of weeks ago, the carnival was thriving with business, but the swamp monster appeared and started scaring off the tourists.

Forced to spend the night, they decide to try to catch the swamp monster. As the leader, Fred comes up with a plan, and his plan is always the same: split up. For some reason, Fred seems to think that "splitting up" is the answer to every crisis on planet Earth. Threat of a nuclear attack? Split up. Terrorist threat? Split up. But once Fred divides up the team, his angle soon becomes apparent. He sends Velma (we'll call her the "plain looking" one) with Shaggy and Scooby, and surprise, surprise, he ends up alone with the hot chick, Daphne.

Shaggy and Scooby spend the majority of the show cowering in the corner or running in fear. In the final parts of the episode, Velma will devise a way-too-complicated plan to capture the monster. A few steps into the plan, Shaggy or Scooby trip over something, mess up the plan, and a comical and chaotic chase ensues, ending with a crash and the monster getting captured. As they remove the mask, spoiler alert, the swamp monster isn't real.

There are too many Shaggy and Scooby Christians: living in fear and running from things that aren't real.

---

There are too many Shaggy and Scooby Christians: living in fear and running from things that aren't real.

---

In fact, if you are facing something in your life that's causing fear, you should actually get excited. Why? Because why would the enemy try to scare you away from something if he didn't know a huge blessing was just on the other side?

Is your child facing some sort of fear? This is a great time to teach them about the tactics of the enemy. Teach them that the enemy is trying to scare them away from a blessing on the other side. Identify the blessing. Identify the falseness of the fear. Pray for the courage of the Holy Spirit to run towards what God has for them on the other side.

Will our kids be defined by what they run FROM? Or what they run TOWARD?
Let's teach them to run toward!

Run toward the unknown.
Run toward risk.
Run toward adventure.
Run toward purpose.
Run with abandon toward Jesus!

When your kids run toward their fears, they're not just running toward their fears, they're running toward their future.

## Run Toward Your Future

David's future was right on the other side of Goliath. Before Goliath, he was a no-name shepherd. After Goliath, he was a household hero and the subject of a top-40 song. Everyone knew David. The battle with Goliath was the launching pad into the fullness of God's purpose for David's life. Goliath got David a wife and a place in the king's palace. Goliath got him wealth and notoriety. We can fairly safe say that without Goliath, David would not have been made king. And he never would have defeated Goliath if he had not run towards Goliath.

David's greatest blessing was right on the other side of his greatest fear.

Your greatest blessing is right on the other side of your greatest fear.

Your children's greatest blessings are right on the other side of their greatest fear.

Your children's greatest blessings are right on the other side of their greatest fear.

This occasion wasn't the only time in his life that David ran toward something. Just after David had been elected king, he was preparing to step in and take the city of Jerusalem. But the Jebusites were living there. As David prepares his troops for battle, the Jebusites realize they are outnumbered and overpowered, so they resort to the battle tactic of fear. The Bible says they begin to taunt King David. "You will not get in here; even the blind and the lame can ward you off."[8] When you are on the verge of stepping into blessing and destiny, the enemy will ramp up his fear tactics in your life too.

David obeys the Lord and, in the face of taunts and fear tactics of the enemy, easily takes the city. He names it Jerusalem, the City of David, which becomes the capital of the greatest nation on Earth in its time.

David was able to dismiss the empty, fear-tactic taunts of the Jebusites because he had dismissed the empty, fear-tactic taunts of Goliath. David ran toward Jerusalem because he had learned to run toward Goliath. When we realize that fears are false and that blessing is on the other side of our fear, we can run with confidence toward our future.

My friend and spiritual mentor, Phil Bennett, describes life on the other side of fear as "a whole new world opening before us."[9] Over the past fifteen or so years, I have seen firsthand how Phil has walked hundreds of people through defeating fear. Phil says, "Like Columbus, a whole new worlds awaits us" on the other side of fear.[10]

## A Surfing Experience

I was preaching in Eastern North Carolina, and the news that week was all about shark attacks. Two attacks had occurred off the coast of Oak Island within 90 minutes of each other on a two-mile stretch of beach. A twelve-year-old and a sixteen-year-old had both survived the attacks, but both had also lost arms. One shark attack is incredibly rare, but two that close to each other within the same time frame is almost unheard of.

Of course, people were freaking out. Facebook was lighting up. "Stay out of the water!" "Sharks are everywhere!" One lady said she hadn't been in the ocean since her husband caught a shark while surf fishing, and that was three years ago! It certainly didn't help that this very week was the 40th anniversary of Jaws.

The problem for me was that in between preaching assignments, I had Saturday off and was planning to visit one of my favorite surf spots at the Outer Banks. I had my surfboard loaded up. But shark talk filled the airwaves and cyberspace. Some fear started to creep in to. But I made up my mind that there was no way I was going to let fear stop me from doing one of my absolute favorite things to do in life—going to the beach and playing in the ocean.

When I pulled my GMC 4x4 truck into Nags Head, the morning was absolutely gorgeous. The sun was out, the air was warm, and the June ocean still had a touch of refreshing coolness to it. A small East, Northeast leftover swell with a light offshore wind was in place. Translation for non-surfers: great longboard conditions. So I paddled out. It was an amazing morning. The sea was like glass. The emerald water was so clear you could see to the bottom. Dolphins were playing. I surfed some great waves, even surfing right over a stingray at one point. It was amazing. I never would have had this experience if I had given in to my fears.

## Facing Parenting Fears

Not only does facing our fears have huge implications for our children, but it does for parents as well. Isn't the source of our fears often, "What if something bad happens to my kid?" I experienced this very thing when getting ready to send my son Cade to summer camp for the first time. He had just completed first grade, and this would be his first time away from home for an extended period of time. You already know that for the past twenty years, I have been involved with summer camps, and you won't find anyone who believes in the destiny-releasing power of summer camp more than I do. But for some reason, I was facing fear. What if something happened to Cade?

They had a lake, and even though Cade was a good swimmer, things happen. The enemy was really working me over.

I knew that the Lord had great things in store for Cade at that camp. I knew the enemy knew that God had great things in store for Cade at that camp. No wonder he was pulling a "Scooby Doo Swamp Monster" on me. We sent Cade. Half way through the week, we snuck in the back of the evening service. Tears rolled down my cheeks as I watched my son raising his hands and worshipping God. It doesn't get much better than that. He never would have had that experience had I succumbed to my fears.

Of course, by "fear" I am not talking about Godly wisdom and concern. "I'm afraid to let my fifteen-year-old princess go out on a date with an eighteen-year-old high school drop-out and stay out until midnight." That's not fear, Dad. That's shotgun-retrieving action stuff!

I'm talking about the kind of fear that the enemy puts into your mind about your kids. "Don't send your kids on a mission trip. Something bad might happen to them." "Don't send your kids away to a Christian college. They'll be better off just staying close to home." "Don't fight Goliath, David. You'll be killed." Those lies are from the pit of hell and are aimed at thwarting the future of your child.

Sometimes we can become paralyzed by fear when we confuse courage with an emotion. Courage is not the absence of fear. Sometimes courage is action in the midst of fear. Courage is facing your fears. Remember David's brothers? The runners? Don't spend your life running from your fears. Decide in your heart not to run away from the very thing that could end up being one of the biggest blessings in your life.

---

Courage is not the absence of fear. Courage is action in the midst of fear.

---

## Run Toward Helping Others

By all accounts, Goliath didn't necessarily disturb David's life on a daily basis. He didn't have any contact with the giant other than running errands for his dad and checking on his brothers. David pretty easily could have had a "that's someone else's problem" attitude, dropped off the care package, and gone back to the serenity of tending sheep. But he didn't.

Yes, David asked what the reward was. I don't want to minimize that reality. The Bible teaches that men and women of God who do God's work with the right heart and spirit should receive proper payment. But I don't think his entire motivation was personal benefit. David was upset that someone dared to defy the name of his God, and I believe that he had a concern for the Israelites. David ran toward Goliath so God would receive the glory and other people would be free.

This pattern of courage for the glory of God and for the sake of others would become the basis of his royal reign as well. When David ran toward the Jebusites, ousting them from his rightful territory, and renaming it the City of David, the Bible says, "Then David knew that the Lord had established him as king over Israel and had exalted his kingdom for the sake of his people Israel."[11] David ran toward Jerusalem so that God would get the glory and other people would benefit.

David lived with one hand pointed upward to heaven and one hand pointed outward to people. He recognized that every blessing in his life was from God and for others. What a great posture for our kids to carry through life—every victory, every blessing, and every good thing they have comes from the Lord and is given for the benefit of others around us.

### A Basketball Hero

I love stories where people display uncommon courage. I especially love when the display of that courage is for someone else's benefit. I came across a YouTube video about Mitchell Marcus, a teenager with developmental disabilities, who served as equipment manager for his high school basketball team, the Coronado Thunderbirds in El Paso, TX.[12] The kid was an absolute delight. He loved basketball. He loved the other kids on the team. And the team loved him. During the last game of the season, his coach Peter Morales surprised Mitchell by allowing him to dress for the game. While that decision alone would have made the kid's year, the coach went a step further by making the decision to put Mitchell in at the end of the game, no matter what the score.

At this point, his teammates stepped up. They started making it their goal for Mitchell to score a goal. They did everything they could to set him up to make just one bucket. While he came close a few times, each attempt missed. On the final play of the game, the other team had the ball for an inbounds play. As the opposing player, senior Jonathan Montañez, stood on the sideline, ball in hand, looking for an open teammate, he saw Mitchell standing in front of him. He made a decision that I'm not sure many players would have made. With only seconds remaining, Jonathan yelled out Mitchell's name. When Mitchell turned, Jonathan passed the ball right to him. Mitchell caught the ball and, as the buzzer went off, made the shot. It may not have been the game winner, but it was a life maker.

After the game, Jonathan simply said, "I was raised to treat others the way you want to be treated. I just thought Mitchell deserved his chance."

What would your child do? What would my child do? I can only hope that he or she would pass the ball to Mitchell.

The Apostle Paul reminds us to "do nothing out of selfish ambition or vain conceit. Rather, in humility value others above yourselves, not looking to your own interests but each of you to the interests of the others."[13] When we teach our kids to have this kind of attitude and posture in life, the life and blessing of God is able to flow through them to others.

## Run in Your Own Armor

David was offered Saul's armor. He turned it down because it didn't fit. When you're raised in the hiddenness of a shepherd's field, you emerge knowing who you are, and you don't have to fight your battles wearing someone else's armor. As a young teenager, David was able to shed easily the pressure of trying to live someone else's life and trying to live out someone else's expectations.

When kids are raised on the stage, they learn to live for applause and for pleasing other people. When the stage lights (or athletic field lights) go off, they're left in the dark. Who they are becomes connected to the talent or ability that they've developed and to how that gift pleases other people. But in the hidden shepherd's field, there's no such pressure. Children learn who they are before they think about what they'll become.

When kids are raised on the stage they learn to live for applause and for pleasing other people. But in the hidden shepherd's field, there's no such pressure. Children learn who they are before they think about what they'll become.

Recently I stood backstage at a national fine arts competition watching thirteen-year-old Macy walk onto stage and sing with beauty, power, and poise. Macy had won the national award of merit in her age group for female vocal solo and was chosen to perform that night in Louisville, KY in front of 11,000 people.

I know this family well. Her father is the worship and arts pastor at a large church and may be one of the most talented and creative people I know. Her mom is a chorus teacher at a local elementary school and is extremely gifted as well. Together they lead a team that puts on musicals and productions not only for the church but for the community. One of their summer ministries is an arts camp for kids that puts on mini Broadway-type musicals.

You might think that with this kind of pedigree, this girl would have been on stage by the time she was five. Not so. Sure, I saw Macy in a couple of performances with smaller roles, but as a child, she was never pushed or thrust into the spotlight. She was allowed to be a little girl. As she grew older and began to develop a passion of her own for the arts, her parents invested in her and, when she was in middle school, they unleashed her on the world. Because Macy was allowed a time of hiddenness as a child, she was able to grow in confidence not only in her abilities but in her own armor. Because she wasn't forced to grow up under stage lights, when she did step onto stage, she possessed the confidence of a young lady who knew who God made her to be.

The number one regret of dying people? *I didn't have the courage to live my own life. I spent my life trying to live the life I thought other people wanted me to live.* When your children are raised in a childhood of hiddenness and innocence, they can emerge knowing who they are in Christ, and they can run with confidence in their own armor. As my friend Steve Hargett says, "God is writing your own story. Don't plagiarize someone else's."

---

The number one regret of dying people? *I didn't have the courage to live my own life. I spent my life trying to live the life I thought other people wanted me to live.*

---

## RUN TOWARD THE FATHER

David certainly ran towards all of the things we have discussed—the real enemy, his fears, his future, and helping others. He could run toward all of these because at the end of the day, he was running toward his Heavenly Father. As Goliath taunted him one final time, David replied,

> "You come against me with sword and spear and javelin, but I come against you in the name of the Lord Almighty, the God of the armies of Israel, whom you have defied. This day the Lord will deliver you into my hands, and I'll strike you down and cut off your head. This very day I will give the carcasses of the Philistine army to the birds and the wild animals, and the whole world will know that there is a God in Israel. All those gathered here will know that it is not by sword or spear that the Lord saves; for the battle is the Lord's, and he will give all of you into our hands."[14]

Notice how many times David refers to the Lord. This declaration wasn't just about David's future or even primarily about helping others. This was about the Lord, the very Father who had raised young David in the hiddenness of the shepherd's field for all those years. When you are close to your Heavenly Father, you care about God. You want God to get the glory. You want God's name to be exalted. And you realize that the battle is God's.

Parents, when you raise your children in the hiddenness of the shepherd's field, they learn to run to their true Father, their Heavenly Father. They learn that every battle, every trial, every obstacle, every hurt, and everything standing in their way are the Lord's battle to fight. They will be able to say, as David did, "All those gathered here will know that it is not by sword or spear that the Lord saves; for the battle is the Lord's, and he will give all of you into our hands." No matter what the future brings, you can raise your kids with the confidence of knowing that "the battle is the Lord's."

## Chris and Carey

I have friends who serve as statewide youth directors for our denomination. They are energetic, full of life, and super friendly. (Except when Chris is on the basketball court, then he turns into an immovable force!) At a conference they attended, a speaker issued a challenge to a packed arena: "Would you be willing to say 'yes' to Jesus before you even knew what the question was?" Chris and Carey both responded to that altar call, and Chris found himself on the floor weeping before the Lord. Even though this couple was actively serving the Lord with all of their hearts, they were sensing a shift in ministry assignment. To what? They didn't know. But whatever it was, they found themselves saying "yes".

Throughout the ensuing weeks and months, as Chris and Carey continued to seek direction from the Lord for their future, they had a deep sense God was calling them to missionary service in the Maldives. While that group of islands may sound familiar as a top tourist destination, it's far from a place you would want to be a missionary. As Chris says, "It may look like paradise, but it's paradise lost." Away from the glitz of the tourist spots, the native parts of the islands have incredibly high drug usage. The nation has the highest divorce rate in the world. Isis recruits more people from there than anywhere in the world. At the time of this writing, not a single known Christian is in the entire nation.

As Chris and Carey began to process the challenges they would face and the difficulty of the new assignment, their concern was not just for themselves, but for their four children. They would be taking their children halfway around the world, away from their church, their friends, their school, and their family. The kids would be in an environment that was, except for their immediate family, completely void of people who follow Jesus. You can imagine the hesitations with which Chris and Carey wrestled.

They decided to take an "appetizer trip". After contacting a missionary friend, the family spent a couple of weeks in adverse conditions in a very poverty-stricken part of India. Their prayer was that if God was calling them, God would call their entire family. Upon their return to the states, they walked by their eight-year-old daughter's room. She had worship music playing and was kneeling by her bed praying and weeping for the children of that part of the world. A few days later, their thoughtful, matter-of-fact twelve-year-old son approached Chris. "Dad, I saw a vision. I saw people line up across the Maldives, and I was preaching to them." When you run toward the Father, He will provide. If God is calling your kids to something, the battle is the Lord's.

I don't know all God is up to in my life, in my wife's life, or in my children's lives. I don't know everything that the future has in store, or even what next week has in store. But I want our family to live with abandon in regards to the love of the Father. I want us to say "yes" to Jesus before we even know what the question is. There is no place more dangerous, *and at the same time more safe,* than in the arms of the Father.

## A Final Blessing

As you finish reading this book, I wonder if you feel the same as I do having written it—both encouraged and discouraged all wrapped together. Encouraged by your faith in God, but discouraged by your own faults and failures. I know I sure still struggle with the latter. I want to remind you (and myself) that God doesn't always raise great kids because of us, but sometimes in spite of us.

My final encouragement would be the words the Lord spoke to Paul two thousand years ago: "'My grace is sufficient for you, for my power is made perfect in weakness.' Therefore I will boast all the more gladly about my weaknesses, so that Christ's power may rest on me."

God's grace is the key. It has always been about God's grace. You can go forward knowing that despite your flaws, Jesus will shine through you. Parents, you got this. Because God's got this.

I bless you to raise kids who love Jesus.
I bless you to raise kids who walk in anointing.
I bless you to raise kids who have a playful spirit.
I bless you to raise kids who choose a faith-adventure.
I bless you to raise kids who are strong.
I bless you to raise kids who are courageous.
May the Lord raise up a generation who loves Jesus, loves life, and lives courageously.

## GROUP DISCUSSION GUIDE

1) Define what the "running from" list looks like for your child(ren). What does it look like for you? Discuss and create a "run to" list for you and your family.
2) Candidly discuss fears you face as a parent. Do you see some of your fears in life transferring toward your child(ren)? What steps can you take to eliminate these fears and be an example to your child(ren) on how to overcome F.E.A.R.?
3) Discuss and then take advantage of opportunities for your child(ren) to "run toward helping others" as they arise.
4) Discuss and implement ways to keep and open dialogue throughout your child(ren)'s lives on how to continually "run toward the Father." Receive the final blessing spoken over you by the author!

# NOTES

## PREFACE

1. Phil Cooke, *One Big Thing: Discovering What You Were Born to Do* (Nashville: Thomas Nelson, 2012), 113.

## CHAPTER 1

1. Ted Cunningham, *Trophy Child* (Colorado Springs, Co.: David C Cook, 2012).

2. Psalm 71:17, NLT.

3. 2 Corinthians 12:9, NIV.

4. 1 Samuel 16:12-13.

## CHAPTER 2

1. Paul Tough, *How Children Succeed: Grit, Curiosity, and the Hidden Power of Character* (New York, NY: Mariner Books, 2012), xiii.

2. Ibid., xv.

3. Jasper Truyen, "Are Performances at Young Age a Good Predictor of Later Success? The Development of a Youth Elite Sport Index." Accessed January 20, 2016. http://www.easm.net/download/2008/08eb574a76940e4e06479dd514552c78.pdf.

4. In other sports, the correlation didn't show up until even later. Take Judo, for instance. An accurate assessment of how good or

successful a young man might be couldn't be determined until his early twenties.

5. Bob Bigelow, Tom Moroney, and Linda Hall. *Just Let the Kids Play: How to Stop Other Adults from Ruining Your Child's Fun and Success in Youth Sports.* Deerfield Beach, FL: Health Communications, 2001, xiv.

6. Ibid., 5.

7. Ibid., 91.

8. Ibid., 92.

9. Bigelow, 22.

10. *Michael Jordan: To the Max.* Produced by James Sternberg, Don Kempf, and Steve Kempf. Performed by Michael Jordan, Phil Jackson, Steve Kerr, Bob Costas. Fox, 2000. DVD.

11. Kobe Bryant recently came down extremely hard on AAU basketball. "AAU basketball," Bryant said. "Horrible, terrible AAU basketball. It's stupid. It doesn't teach our kids how to play the game at all so you wind up having players that are big and they bring it up and they do all this fancy crap and they don't know how to post. They don't know the fundamentals of the game. It's stupid." Arash Markazi, "Kobe: Europe's Players More Skillful," ESPN, January 3, 2015, section goes here, accessed April 27, 2016, http://espn.go.com/losangeles/nba/story/_/id/12114523/kobe-bryant-says-european-players-more-skilled-americans-blames-aau.

12. Mark Koba, "Spending Big on Kids' Sports? You're Not Alone," CNBC, January 13, 2014, accessed February 12, 2016, http://www.cnbc.com/2014/01/13/youth-sports-is-a-7-billion-industry-and-growing.html.

13. Caitlin Wheeler, "Sports Travel Teams: Option or Necessity," *Piedmont Parent*, October 2015, 11.

14. Minnesota Amateur Sports Commission, Athletic Footwear Association, USA Today Survey, Michigan State

15. https://www.ncaa.org/sites/default/files/Probability-of-going-pro-methodology_Update2013.pdf

16. http://www.usyouthsoccer.org/media_kit/keystatistics/

17. Calculations are made with the base of $2266 and adding $2266 yearly for ten years, in an ESA yielding a ten percent average annual return.

18. "Scientists have reached a consensus in the past decade that the key channel through which early adversity causes damage to developing bodies and brains is *stress*." Paul Tough, *How Children Succeed,* (New York: Mariner Books, 2012), 10-11.

19. Tough, pp. 12-13.

20. Scarlet, Janina. "'Inside Out': Emotional Truths by Way of Pixar." Psychology Today. Accessed December 14, 2015. https://www.psychologytoday.com/blog/beyond-heroes-and-villains/201506/inside-out-emotional-truths-way-pixar.

21. Chap Clark, *Hurt 2.0: Inside the World of Today's Teenagers* (Grand Rapids, MI: Baker Academic, 2011), p. 108.

22. Chap Clark, *Hurt 2.0: Inside the World of Today's Teenagers* (Grand Rapids, MI: Baker Academic, 2011).

23. Clark, 112.

24. Wendy Mogel, *The Blessing of a Skinned Knee* (New York: Scribner, 2001).

25. Matthew 18:3-5, NIV.

26. Matthew 18:6-9, NIV.

27. *The Hunger Games* (Roadshow, 2012).

## CHAPTER 3

1. Jacque Wilson, "Choir Singers' Hearts Beat as One," The Chart RSS, July 8, 2013, accessed April 28, 2014, http://thechart.blogs.cnn.com/2013/07/08/choir-singers-hearts-beat-as-one/.

2. Leonard Sweet, *From Tablet to Table: Where Community Is Found and Identity Is Formed* (Colorado Springs, CO: NavPress, 2014), p. 12.

3. William Mancini. "The Most Disturbing Church Trend of Them All." Charisma News. Accessed December 14, 2015. http://www.charismanews.com/us/47835-the-most-disturbing-church-trend-of-them-all. Mancini goes on to state that one reason for this is "Increasing involvement with kids' activities including more

'multiple activity' commitments (sports, music, etc.) for longer duration with greater competitiveness. The growth of club sports and the intensity of competition creates a market for kids to get started earlier and be involved longer. This is literally eating our families alive when it comes to time."

* I do realize that not all children connect with the "largeness" of a summer camp setting. For some, a smaller youth group retreat may be more conducive to their personality. What is important is that we invest in Bethel moments for our children, regardless of exactly how they may look.

## CHAPTER 4

1. Joshua 3:5, NIV.

2. This is a paraphrase of Jesus' prayer for his disciples in John. "I have given them your word and the world has hated them, for they are not of the world any more than I am of the world. My prayer is not that you take them out of the world but that you protect them from the evil one. They are not of the world, even as I am not of it. Sanctify them by the truth; your word is truth. As you sent me into the world, I have sent them into the world. For them I sanctify myself, that they too may be truly sanctified (John 17:14-17, NIV).

3. Matthew 5:27-28, NIV.

4. Ephesians 5:3, NIV.

5. Zechariah 3:1-4, NLT.

6. Zechariah 3:2.

7. Acts 2:14-19, NIV.

## CHAPTER 5

1. Strong's Hebrew. Bible Hub. Accessed October 08, 2015. http://biblehub.com/hebrew/119.htm.

2. Strong's Hebrew. Bible Hub. Accessed October 08, 2015.http://biblehub.com/hebrew/132.htm

3. Cheryl Charles and Richard Louv. "Children's Nature Deficit: What We Know and Don't Know." *Children and Nature Network*, September 2009, 1-68. Accessed February 2015. childrenandnature.org/research., pp. 1-2.

4. Ibid., p. 4.

5. Peter Gray, Ph.D., "The Decline of Play and Rise in Children's Mental Disorders," Psychology Today, January 26, 2010, accessed May 02, 2016, https://www.psychologytoday.com/blog/freedom-learn/201001/the-decline-play-and-rise-in-childrens-mental-disorders#_=_.

6. Cheryl Charles and Richard Loud, "Children's Nature Deficit: What We Know and Don't Know," *Children and Nature Network*, September 2009, p. 4, http://childrenandnature.org.

7. Stuart L. Brown, *Play: How It Shapes the Brain, Opens the Imagination, and Invigorates the Soul,* (New York: Avery, 2009).

8. Charles and Louv, p. 5.

9. Christopher Connelly, "Turns Out Monkey Bars And Kickball Might Be Good For The Brain," NPR, January 3, 2016, accessed April 27, 2016, http://www.npr.org/sections/ed/2016/01/03/460254858/turns-out-monkey-bars-and-kickball-are-good-for-the-brain.

10. Ibid.

11. Devin Brown, *Tolkien: How an Obscure Oxford Professor Wrote The Hobbit and Became the Most Beloved Author of the Century* (Nashville, TN: Abingdon Press, 2014).

## CHAPTER 6

1. *The Thousand Year Journey: Oregon to Patagonia.* Directed by Kenny Laubbacher. Accessed January 26, 2016. https://vimeo.com/search?q=the+thousand+year+journey+oregon+to+patagonia.

2. Genesis 1:28, NLT.

3. Jones goes on to say, "The teacher's task consisted of preparing the needed knowledge by organizing it in a linear way, imposing an interpretation on the knowledge, and finally transferring it directly to the learner. Because the lecture method was heralded as the highest form of teaching, talking heads that dished out what they thought the public needed to know became the norm." (Paula Champion-Jones, *Brain-Based Worship: Remembering the Mind-Body Connection* [Bloomington, IN: WestBow Press, 2014], 33.

4. Psalm 19:1, NIV.

5. *The Breakfast Club*, dir. John Hughes, perf. Emilio Estevez and Molly Ringwald (1985), film.

6. Michael Hyatt, "The Secret to Ben Carson's Success." Accessed January 20, 2016. https://michaelhyatt.com/ben-carson-reading.html.

7. Dr. Seuss, *I Can Read with My Eyes Shut* (London: HarperCollins Publishers, 2003).

8. Steven James Henderson, "The Impact of Student Religion and College Affiliation on Student Religiosity" (PhD diss., University of Arkansas, 2003), accessed May 2, 2016, http://www.christian-consulting.net/statistics/Dissertation.pdf.

## CHAPTER 7

1. Kevin Miller, Tom Ziglar, and John O'Leary, "John O'Leary Says We All Have Trials. Now What?" *Ziglar's True Performance Show* (audio podcast), July 7, 2016.

2. Christopher McDougall, *Born to Run: A Hidden Tribe, Superathletes, and the Greatest Race the World Has Never Seen* (New York: Alfred A. Knopf, 2009).

3. Bryan Greeson, "Move Over Helicopter Parents, Meet the Lawnmower Parents." *Gaston Gazette*, November 30, 2015. http://www.gastongazette.com/article/20151130/NEWS/151139937.

4. According to Mischel, "The message here is that parents who over-control their toddlers risk undermining the development of their

children's self-control skills, while those who support and encourage autonomy in problem-solving efforts are likely to maximize their children's chances of coming home from preschool eager to tell them how they got two marshmallows." Walter Mischel, *The Marshmallow Test* (New York, NY: Little, Brown, and Company, 2014), 61.

5. Jesse had eight sons (1 Sam 18:12). The oldest three were 20 and older according to Numbers 1:3. At the youngest, the three oldest sons would have been 22, 21, and 20 (unless they were triplets and all twenty years old). The fourth oldest son didn't serve in the army, which means at the oldest, he would have to be 19. That leaves the five sons who didn't join the military to be 19, 18, 17, 16, and 15 assuming that David's mother had one son a year. It's also a possibility that David had elder twin brothers, which would potentially make him older than 15. Kent Owen, http://www.biblebro.net/how-old-was-david/

6. This is an adaptation from a quote I have heard from Len Sweet: "Our churches should not be places safe from risk, but places where it is safe to risk."

7. Psalm 34:18, NIV.

8. Wendy Mogel, *The Blessing of a Skinned Knee: Using Jewish Teachings to Raise Self-Reliant Children* (New York: Scribner, 2001),

9. Ibid., 32.

10. Ibid., 91.

11. Romans 5:3, NIV.

12. Dr. Karen Oberhauser, The Monarch Butterfly. https://www.learner.org/jnorth/search/MonarchNotes2.html, accessed 8 July, 2014.

13. Carol S. Dweck, *Mindset: The New Psychology of Success* (New York: Random House, 2006).

14. Dweck, 92-93.

15. Romans 8:37-39, NIV.

16. Author's paraphrase of Daniel 3:25.

17. Jessica Holzer, "German Kindergarten Campouts Test Helicopter Parents," WSJ, December 28, 2015, accessed February 18, 2016, http://www.wsj.com/articles/german-kindergarten-campouts-test-helicopter-parents-1451338940.

18. Isaiah 54:13

19. John 20:17, NLT.

20. Mogul, p. 43.

21. Ted Cunningham, *Trophy Child.*

## CHAPTER 8

1. 1 Samuel 17:24.

2. 1 Samuel 17:48.

3. Matthew 10:28, NIV.

4. The Human Right is a theme launched by the Assemblies of God. www.thehumanright.org

5. C.S. Lewis, *The Last Battle* (New York, NY: Harper Collins, 1956).

6. 1 Peter 5:8.

7. 1 Peter 5:8; Revelation 5:5.

8. 2 Samuel 5:6, NIV.

9. Phil Bennett, *Spiritual Healing: Breaking the Spider Web of Lies*, (Concord, NC, 2015).

10. Ibid.

11. 1 Samuel 5:12, NIV.

12. Steve Hartman, "High School Basketball Player Passes Ball to Mentally Challenged Player on the Other Team." YouTube. Accessed March 02, 2016. https://www.youtube.com/watch?v=e4zRJIp2wcM. Via CBS News.

13. Philippians 2:3-4, NIV.

14. 1 Samuel 17:45-47, NIV.